Mary

AND

Martha Washington.

Engraved by Rice & Buttre.

Martha Washington

MEMOIRS

OF THE

MOTHER AND WIFE

OF

WASHINGTON.

BY

MARGARET C. CONKLING,

AUTHOR OF HARPERS' TRANSLATION OF "FLORIAN'S HISTORY OF THE MOORS OF SPAIN;" "ISABEL, OR TRIALS OF THE HEART;" ETC., ETC.

"Of differing themes the veering song was mix'd."

"To teach us how divine a thing
A woman may be made."

SECOND EDITION, REVISED AND ENLARGED.

AUBURN:
DERBY, MILLER, AND COMPANY.

1850.

STEREOTYPED BY THOMAS B. SMITH,
216 WILLIAM STREET, N. Y.

TO

MRS. WILLIAM H. SEWARD,

A SLIGHT TRIBUTE TO HER MANY VIRTUES,

AND

IN TOKEN OF HIGH REGARD,

THIS VOLUME

IS VERY RESPECTFULLY INSCRIBED.

THANKS for the picture of thy daily life—
Thy bright example, Daughter, Mother, Wife!
The watchful care that cheers thy sire's decline,
As a lone shaft's long shielded by a vine,
A gentle, holy lesson, graven deep,
Thy daughter, cherished in her heart, will keep;
Thy couch of suffering she 'll bend above,
And soothe thee, ever, with devoted love.
Constant to thee, thy sons will crown thy days
With reverence, heart-felt blessings, fondest praise;
And HE, still proving the truest of friends,
The *homage of whose faith* on thee attends,
Wherever tossed 'mid life's tumultuous jar,
E'er turn to thee, his fixed, his guiding star,
And in thy smile benign, confiding seek
The peace, the happiness, thy prayers bespeak!—
When thou in Heaven dost fold thy spirit-wing,
Around thy name will sweetest memories cling,
Soft as the balmy breath of fragrance cast
On earthly bowers, where Peri's wing has pass'd,

Or radiance ling'ring round the glowing West,
When day serene has gently sunk to rest!

Long may Columbia's Daughters thus portray
The lofty virtue of her earlier day!—
And may the blessings of thy heart and hearth
Change but for those of bright, empyreal birth!

M. C. C.

Melrose, January 1st, 1850.

MEMOIR

OF

MARY WASHINGTON.

Life is not lost, from which is brought
Endless renown. SPENCER.

. . . Virtue, on no aid extraneous bent,
Is to herself, her own bright ornament.
TASSO.

CONTENTS

OF THE

LIFE OF MARY WASHINGTON.

CHAPTER III.

CHAPTER IV.

CHAPTER V.

CHAPTER VI.

CHAPTER VII.

CHAPTER VIII.

THE MOTHER OF WASHINGTON.

INTRODUCTION.

HERE WOMAN REIGNS; the mother, daughter, wife,—
Strews with fresh flowers the narrow way of life;
In the clear heaven of her delightful eye,
An angel guard of loves and graces lie;
Around her knees domestic duties meet,
And fireside pleasures gambol at her feet.

MONTGOMERY.

THE artist who would embody the sublime IDEAL which has long engrossed his spiritual contemplation—the idol of his ceaseless adoration, the imaginary impersonation of his most exalted conceptions of the Beautiful—again and again shrinks dismayed, despairing, from the impossible achievement he would fain essay. Thus does the biographer, whose best qualification for the task too partial friendship has assigned her, is profound reverence for the theme,—approach the awe-inspiring subject of the following Memoir.

The life of woman, almost in proportion as it is true to the loftiest impulses and purest principles by which she can be actuated, presents comparatively few incidents claiming circumstantial record or remembrance.

Though the wife, or the mother of one who fills a large space in the world's eye, it is still, usually, hers to dwell only within the quiet precincts of domestic retirement.

The Hero, like a majestic river, that bears the wealth of cities on its ample waters, and diffuses benefits to thousands, speeds onward in his high career, his steps resounding in the ears of listening nations; while the mother, from whom, perchance, he derived the intellectual power that impels and sustains this lofty course, still, like a life-giving fountain whose sweet, bright waters diffuse beauty, and health, and happiness, lingers ever in the shade, revered in the protecting sanctity of *Home*.

The world may never know, may never seek, the gushing waters of the secluded fountain. But beside its peace-breathing murmurs, the worn and weary wanderer,—fame-pilgrim though he be, seeks repose; returning once more, and yet once more, to imbibe its benign and soothing influences. In the quiet haunt it loves, dwell gentle spirits who minister to the wayfarer, and watch, with ceaseless care, over the sequestered purity and loveliness, which it is their precious charge forever to preserve, in inexhaustible and unsullied perfection.

As flow the crystal waters of a hallowed well-spring, glided on the life of MARY WASHINGTON; thus serene, and pure, and secluded, thus genial and beneficent, and blessed!

CHAPTER I.

> The name of Mary—how the heart
>   Thrills at the sound of that sweet name!
> The holiest thoughts it may impart,
>   Or wake the soul to deeds of fame! — J. W M.

> Well-ordered home, man's best delight to make,
> And with submissive wisdom, modest skill,
> To raise the virtues—— — THOMPSON.

MRS. MARY WASHINGTON was born in the Colony of Virginia, towards the conclusion of the year 1706. Little is known of her ancestors, except that she inherited an unimpeachable name. We are informed that she was descended from a highly respectable family of English colonists, named Ball, who originally established themselves on the banks of the Potomac.

It is to be lamented that no records of the youth, or early womanhood of this illustrious lady have been preserved.

We are, therefore, in ignorance of the education and domestic influences by which her remarkable character was developed and matured.

But judging from the rare combination of mental and moral qualities which we find exhibited in the brief history of her later life, we may suppose her home education to have been particularly practical and judicious; such, indeed, was almost the only instruction received by women in this country, even at a much later period than that to which we refer.

To the abiding effect of early maternal training, Mrs. Washington must have been, at least in some degree, indebted for her habits of unusual industry, economy, and regularity, as well as for the excellent constitution, that gave vigor and practical usefulness to the operations of a naturally powerful intellect. To the ineffaceable impressions of infant years, we may also ascribe the moral elevation and the exalted piety associated with her noble mind.

Augustine Washington, the husband of the celebrated subject of our Memoir, was a gentleman of considerable wealth, and of distinguished lineage and position. Several of his ancestors early emigrated to the Colony of Virginia, and honorable mention is made of more than one of them in the annals of the primitive days of the Old Dominion.*

* Everything relating, even remotely, to the history of Wash-

"His occupation was that of a planter, which, from the first settlement of the country, had been the pursuit of nearly all the principal gentlemen of Virginia."

Little can now be definitely ascertained respecting the individual character of the father of the great American Hero. His premature death, and the entire want of any minute family record respecting him, render research in relation to his personal history almost wholly futile. We can only infer his worth from the distinct remembrance in which his paternal tenderness was always held by his most eminent descendant, and from the fact that the valuable estate he possessed at his death, was "chiefly acquired by his own industry and enterprise, which would seem to indicate that in the concerns of business, he was methodical, skilful, honorable, and energetic."*

Mr. Washington was twice married. Two sons survived his first union. He was united to Mary Ball on the 6th of March, 1730.

ington, is so generally interesting, that we append, for the convenience of the curious in such matters, Mr. Sparks' brief but clear exposition of the genealogy of his father's family. *See Appendix—Note A.*

* Sparks' LIFE OF WASHINGTON.

After her marriage, Mrs. Washington's first residence was in Westmoreland County, Virginia, not far from the beautiful river with which so many of the most agreeable reminiscences of her childhood and youth were associated.

In this, the first home of her wedded life, two years subsequent to the union that promised such exalted and continued felicity, George, her eldest son, was born.

Soon after this event, Mr. Washington removed with his family, "to an estate owned by him in Stafford County, Virginia, on the east side of the Rappahannoc River, opposite Fredericksburg."

As years sped on, Mrs. Washington became the mother of two daughters, and three sons. She had thus, six children:—these were successively, George, Betty, Samuel, John Augustine, Charles, and Mildred. The latter died in infancy.

We discover no positive proof that the elder sons of her husband were under the immediate care of Mrs. Washington, but as many incidental indications present themselves of the cordial affection, unity and interest that existed, in later years, among the members of the family, collectively, we may believe, especially in connection with the strong sense of duty which, apparently, characterized every action of this faithful wife and mother, that her native benevolence and justice were not at fault in this instance.

The domestic happiness of this interesting little circle was soon most painfully and unexpectedly interrupted. A short and sudden illness terminated the life of Mr. Washington, on the 12th of April, 1743, at the age of forty-nine years.

In the brief biographical notices of Mrs. Washington which have, hitherto, appeared, she is represented as being left by the death of her husband with very limited pecuniary resources. The testimony of Mr. Sparks,—than which nothing can well be more accurate and incontrovertible,—militates, most emphatically, against the impression thus generally expressed. The following passages contain Mr. Sparks' statement upon this subject:—"It appears by his will that he [Mr. W.] possessed a large and valuable property in lands." * * * * * * *

"Each of his sons inherited from him a separate plantation. To the eldest, Lawrence, he bequeathed an estate near Hunting Creek, afterwards Mount Vernon, which then consisted of twenty-five hundred acres; and also other lands, and shares in iron-works situated in Virginia and Maryland, which were productive. The second son had for his part an estate in Westmoreland. To George were left the lands and mansion where his father lived at the time of his decease; and to each of the other sons an estate of six or seven hundred acres. The youngest daughter died when an infant, and for the only remaining one a suitable provision was made in the will. It is thus seen that Augustine Washington, although suddenly cut off in the vigor of manhood, left all his children in a state of comparative independence. Confiding in the prudence of the mother, he directed that the proceeds of all the property of her children should be at her disposal, till they should respectively come of age."

It was now that the extraordinary characteristics of this exemplary matron began most strikingly to exhibit themselves.

Gifted with great firmness and constancy of purpose, as well as with a clear, discriminating judgment, and remarkable mental independence, her self-reliance was rapidly strengthened, and soon rendered habitual, by circumstances so peculiarly demanding its exercise, as those ir which duty imperatively summoned her to act.

Her thorough knowledge of practical life enabled her not only to superintend, in person, the complicated and important pecuniary affairs of her children, and the general interests of her household, but, also, by her indefatigable industry and ingenuity to supply, in a good degree, whatever was necessary to the welfare and comfort of her family.

Mrs. Washington had, henceforth, the exclusive direction of the primary education of her children. At once their companion, mentor, counsellor, and friend, she encouraged them to mental exertion, to moral culture, to athletic exercise. She taught them self-respect, respect for the rights and feelings of others, self-control, and patience under fatigue and suffering; she stimulated in them a fondness for labor and for knowledge; she inspired them with affection for each other, and for their country, and with the fear and love of God. In short, it was her systematic and unceasing endeavor, to illustrate and enforce willing compliance with the all-wise and immutable laws by which the physical, intellectual, and moral nature of man should be, harmoniously and unitedly, governed. Thus order, regularity, and occupation, sympathy, cheerfulness, and unity, reigned supreme among the youthful denizens of her little world of home. She exacted implicit obedience from her children, and she tempered maternal tenderness by strict domestic discipline; but we are told by one* who, as the companion of her son, occasionally shared her care and hospitality, that she was "indeed truly kind."

In that genuine and judicious kindness lies the secret of the power always maintained by this venerated mother over the minds of her offspring. If she assumed the right to direct the actions of others, her daily life exhibited such powers of self-control and self-denial as convinced her children, by more irresistible evidence than mere words could convey, of the justice and disinterestedness by which she was habitually actuated.

That she rendered their home, simple, nay even

* Laurence Washington, Esq., of Chotank, who thus described his distinguished relative: "I was often there with George, his playmate, schoolmate, and young man's companion. Of the mother I was more afraid than of my own parents; she awed me in the midst of her kindness, for she was indeed truly kind; and even now, when time has whitened my locks, and I am the grandfather of a second generation, I could not behold that majestic woman without feelings it is impossible to describe."

humble, though it might be, endearing to her children, is proved in some degree, by the frequency and pleasure with which, as we gather from much incidental testimony, the happy band that once rejoiced in the comfort and security of her well-ordered abode, in after years revisited the maternal roof. Indeed, we are expressly informed, upon the best authority, that an interdiction of the innocent amusements and relaxations, a taste for which is so natural to the young, formed no part of the system of juvenile training practised with such preëminent success by Mrs. Washington.

She never rendered necessary restraint and discipline needlessly distasteful or repulsive by ascetic sternness or harsh compulsion. The power that sometimes gently coerced the subjects of her guidance was a *moral suasion* far more effective and beneficial than influences such as those can ever exert.

Of all the mental qualities of this celebrated woman, perhaps none was more constantly illustrated in her life than her native *good sense*, the practical effects of which were infinitely more useful and precious to her children than she could possibly have rendered volumes of theoretical precept, however philosophical and profound.

To her possession of this unpretending, but invaluable characteristic, emphatically, her illustrious son was indebted for the education that formed the basis of his greatness.

This it was that taught the great WASHINGTON those habits of application, industry, and regularity, that were of such essential service to him, alike in the camp and in the cabinet, and which so materially contributed to render his character a perfect model, bequeathed to successive ages.

This it was, that, by inculcating and enforcing habitual temperance, exercise, and activity, strengthened and developed the wonderful physical powers that were rivalled only by the indomitable will and stupendous wisdom of her son.

To his mother Washington owed the high value he attached to "*the only possession of which all men are prodigal, and of which all men should be covetous*:" and from her early instructions he imbibed that *love of truth* for which he was remarkable, and which is so pleasingly and forcibly illustrated in some of the favorite anecdotes of our childhood.*

* Our juvenile readers can scarcely fail to be familiar with

Trained to unvarying respect for the truths of revealed religion, in which she was herself a firm believer, and rigidly regardful of the dictates of an enlightened conscience, her gifted son was indebted to Mrs. Washington for his quick moral sense, and the unflinching adhesion to principle that so strongly marked every act of his public and private life.

The noble friend and pupil of Washington, and others among her numerous panegyrists, have likened the mother of the "Hero" to a Spartan matron. With due deference to the high source whence the comparison emanated, it seems scarcely just to her who was its subject. Her life reminds us rather, of those celebrated women whose names are recorded with grateful affection and respect by St. Paul, in his Epistles,—those heroic, self-sacrificing friends and champions of early Christianity, and its devoted advocates, who were "succorers of many," who scorned not to "bestow much labor" upon the temporal necessities of the Apostle and his fellow-martyrs, and

the stories of "The Little Hatchet," and of "The Sorrel Colt," almost the only authentic anecdotes of the childhood of the great American hero, and which also incidentally illustrate *more than one* of his youthful habits.

who even "laid down their own necks" for them! Mrs. Washington was a CHRISTIAN MATRON, who derived her ideas of parental authority and government from the same BOOK, wherein she sought her own rules of life; and she was as much superior to a Spartan mother, as are the inspired principles of our blessed religion to the heathen teachings which exalted mere physical courage above the highest virtues of humanity!

CHAPTER II.

> 'T is the Divinity that stirs within us! ADDISON.

> ——Must such minds be nourish'd in the wild,
> Deep in the upturned forests, midst the roar
> Of cataracts, where nursing Nature smiled
> On infant Washington? Has earth no more
> Such seed within her breast and Europe no such shore?
> BYRON.

WE are unable to present our readers with any particulars of the life of MRS. WASHINGTON, for several years previous to the American Revolution, except such as are gleaned from the published accounts of those troubled times, as associated with the history of her son.

The incipient workings of the mighty spirit destined to achievements that should move the world, influenced the youthful Washington, when only fourteen years of age, to form plans for independent efforts in a more enlarged sphere of exertion than was afforded him by the employment and duties of home life. He had actually taken the necessary steps preliminary to entering the English Navy, when the disapproval of his mother prevented the accomplishment of his design.

Our readers will be interested in the details respecting this incident furnished by Mr. Sparks:

Washington's "eldest brother,* Lawrence, had been an officer in the late war, and served at the siege of Carthagena and in the West Indies. Being a well-informed and accomplished gentleman, he had acquired the esteem and confidence of General Wentworth and Admiral Vernon, the commanders of the expedition, with whom he afterwards kept up a friendly correspondence. Having observed the military turn of his young brother, and looking upon the British Navy as the most direct road to distinction in that line, he obtained for George a midshipman's warrant, in the year 1746, when he was fourteen years old. This step was taken with his acquiescence, if not at his request, and he prepared with a buoyant spirit for his departure; but, as the time approached, the solicitude of his mother interposed with an authority, to which nature gave a claim."

"At this critical juncture, Mr. Jackson, a friend

* The eldest son of Augustine Washington.

of the family, wrote to Lawrence Washington as follows: 'I am afraid Mrs. Washington will not keep up her first resolution. She seems to dislike George's going to sea, and says, several persons have told her it was a bad scheme. She offers several trifling objections, such as fond unthinking mothers habitually suggest; and I find that one word against his going has more weight than ten for it.' She persisted in opposing the plan, and it was given up. Nor ought that decision to be ascribed to obstinacy, or maternal weakness. It was her eldest son, whose character and manners must already have exhibited a promise, full of solace and hope to a widowed mother, on whom alone devolved the charge of four younger children. To see him separated from her at so tender an age, exposed to the perils of accident and the world's rough usage, without a parent's voice to counsel or a parent's hand to guide, and to enter on a theatre of action, which would forever remove him from her presence, was a trial of her fortitude and sense of duty, which she could not be expected to hazard without reluctance and concern."*

Chief Justice Marshall's version of the matter

* Sparks' LIFE OF WASHINGTON, vol. i. p. 10.

ascribes rather a more active personal agency to Washington himself, than that of Mr. Sparks. He says:—

"Those powerful attractions which the profession of arms presents to young and ardent minds, possessed their full influence over Mr Washington. Stimulated by the enthusiasm of military genius, to take part in the war in which Great Britain was then engaged, he had pressed so earnestly to enter the navy, that, at the age of fifteen, a midshipman's warrant was obtained for him."*

But the numerous biographers of Washington, however they may differ in other respects, agree in ascribing his abandonment of this cherished scheme to the all-powerful influence of his mother. One of them affirms that the luggage of the young enthusiast was actually conveyed on board the little vessel destined to bear him away to his new post, and that, when he attempted to bid adieu to his only parent, his previous resolution to depart was for the first time subdued, in consequence of her ill-concealed dejection and her irrepressible tears.

Who shall say that the decisive interposition

* Marshall's LIFE OF WASHINGTON, vol. i. p. 2.

of his mother did not save from a life of limited usefulness and comparative obscurity, the embryo soldier and statesman!

Mrs. Washington proved the injustice of the imputation of weak, maternal fondness, which as we have seen was so erroneously supposed, by at least one of her friends, to be the source of her opposition to the wishes of her son, by the cheerfulness with which, almost immediately after the abandonment of his original design, she relinquished the pleasure and benefit she would have derived from his continued residence under the paternal roof.

Juvenile as he was for assuming an occupation involving responsibilities so serious, the incipient hero was soon actively engaged in the profession of engineering, for which his favorite intellectual pursuits and his taste for athletic exercise had already prepared him. In consequence of the near vicinity of the residence of his half-brother, Lawrence, to the principal scene of his operations, George became an inmate of his family, and continued, thenceforth, to be an absentee from his early home, with only the brief exceptions made by his being occasionally and temporarily there to aid in the care and arrangement of his mother's affairs.

A few years after his first withdrawal from her immediate personal guidance, this self-sacrificing parent was, for several successive months, deprived of even the incidental presence and society of almost the only one of her children who was sufficiently mature to be a congenial and intelligent companion and assistant in her complicated and multitudinous avocations and duties. Mr. Lawrence Washington was compelled by indisposition to seek the more genial climate of Barbadoes, upon the approach of the winter that followed the completion of the nineteenth year of his brother George, whom he selected as the friend and nurse who should accompany him in his voyage, and remain with him after his arrival at his destination. Despite the care and kindness of his amiable attendant, the invalid returned to Virginia in the following spring, to yield himself a victim to the disease that had impelled him to leave home. Subsequent to this sad event, the youthful George, as one of the executors of his will, was long detained from his earlier home by his needful care of the estate and family of his deceased brother.

Mrs. Washington, ever too disinterestedly anxious for the true welfare and happiness of her son, willingly to interpose the slightest obstacle in the high and honorable path which circumstances and his own aspirations and exertions combined to mark out for him, most uncomplainingly and unselfishly resigned the gratification and assistance she would have derived from his residence with her, to promote his present and ulterior advantage.

The lapse of years gradually diminished the imperative exertions and high duties to which Mrs. Washington, during the prime of her womanhood, had so ceaselessly consecrated all the powers of her being. Her eldest daughter assumed the cares and responsibilities of wedded life, and was established in the new home, which wise maternal training had well fitted her to adorn; George, when not engaged in his professional avocations, resided upon the patrimonial estate of Mount Vernon, to which he became heir after the death of the only child of Mr. Lawrence Washington; and the remaining children were rapidly advancing beyond the necessity of that unsleeping vigilance by which the safety, health, and happiness of their earlier days had been so effectually secured.

Some years later, when the young Virginian

who was destined, eventually, to fill so large a space in the world's eye, commenced his initiatory military career, in the service of his native state, we sympathize in the maternal anxiety awakened at once for his personal safety and for his success in arms.

The only letters addressed to his mother, included in the published collection of Washington's Correspondence, were written during the French War, in the earliest stages of which, as our readers will remember, he acted as Adjutant of the northern division of Virginia militia, and as Aid-de-Camp to General Braddock. The first of these was penned just after the memorable and disastrous battle of the Monongahela, at which nothing but the unconquerable determination, that not even severe illness could subdue, enabled the author to be present; and where, if he won some of his proudest laurels, he was, perhaps, exposed to greater personal danger than during any subsequent part of his military career.

Distressing as are the details it contains, we include this letter in our Memoir, entire; not only as one of the two communications, to which we have alluded, but to assist the reader in forming a more correct idea than words of ours could convey, of the dignified and confidential intercourse that was uninterruptedly maintained between these distinguished correspondents.

"To Mrs. Mary Washington, near Fredericksburg.

"Fort Cumberland, 18 July, 1755.

"Honored Madam:

"As I doubt not but you have heard of our defeat, and, perhaps, had it represented in a worse light, if possible, than it deserves, I have taken this earliest opportunity to give you some account of the engagement as it happened, within ten miles of the French Fort, on Wednesday, the 9th instant.

"We marched to that place, without any considerable loss, having only now and then a straggler picked up by the French and scouting Indians. When we came there, we were attacked by a party of French and Indians, whose number, I am persuaded, did not exceed three hundred men; while ours consisted of about one thousand three hundred well-armed troops, chiefly regular soldiers, who were struck with such a panic, that they behaved with more cowardice than it is possible to conceive. The officers behaved gallantly, in order to encourage their men, for which they suffered greatly, there being nearly sixty killed and wounded—a large portion of the number we had.

"The Virginia troops showed a good deal of bravery, and were nearly all killed; for I believe, out of three companies that were there, scarcely thirty men were left alive. Captain Peyrouny, and all his officers, down to a corporal, were killed. Captain Polson had nearly as hard a fate, for only one of his was left. In short, the dastardly behavior of those they call regulars, exposed all others that were inclined to do their duty, to almost certain death; and at last, in despite of all the efforts of the officers to the contrary, they ran as sheep pursued by dogs, and it was impossible to rally them.

"The General was wounded, of which he died three days after. Sir Peter Halkes was killed in the field, where died many other brave officers. I luckily escaped without a wound, though I had four bullets through my coat and two horses shot under me. Captains Orme and Morris, two of the aids-de-camp, were wounded early in the engagement, which rendered the duty harder upon me, as I was the only one then left to distribute the General's orders, which I was scarcely able to do, as I was not half recovered from a violent illness, that had confined me to my bed, and a waggon for ten days. I am still in a weak and feeble condition, which induces me to halt here two or three days, in the hope of recovering a little strength, to enable me to proceed homewards;* from whence I fear I shall not be able to stir till towards September; so that I shall not have the pleasure of seeing you, till then, unless it be in Fairfax. Please to give my love to Mr. Lewis and my sister; and compliments to Mr. Jackson, and all other friends that inquire after me.

"I am, most honored Madam,

"Your most dutiful son."†

We learn from other sources of information, that the indisposition of which the writer so briefly speaks, in this epistle, was sufficiently serious to endanger his life. Nor can we believe his own intimation to have conveyed the first knowledge of this distressing intelligence to his mother. She had, however, the consolation to be, at the same time, informed of all that she

* The reader will remember that Col. W. had already resided some time upon his patrimonial estate of Mount Vernon.

† Sparks' Life of Washington.

could hope or even desire, in relation to his personal prowess and military skill.*

The remaining letter was written in anticipation of an event which occurred soon after the Battle of the Monongahela—the appointment of Colonel Washington to the chief command of the Virginia forces. His commission bears the same date as that of the letter, though the author, as will be seen, was, as yet, uninformed of his promotion.

"To Mrs. Mary Washington.

"Mount Vernon, 14 August, 1755.

"Honored Madam:

"If it is in my power to avoid going to the Ohio again I shall, but if the command is pressed upon me, by the general voice of the country, and offered upon such terms as cannot be objected against, it would reflect dishonor upon me to refuse it. And that, I am sure, ought to give you greater uneasiness than my going in an honor-

* It need scarcely be said that this was the celebrated engagement in which Col. Washington gained so much honor, and the disastrous result of which was nearly averted by his daring courage, as it also might have been by his ready discernment and sagacious tactics, had Gen. Braddock been guided by his advice in the incipient stages of the conflict.

able command. Upon no other terms will I accept of it. At present, I have no proposals made to me, nor have I any advice of such an intention, except from private hands.

"I am, &c."*

Our readers will not fail to remark the almost deprecatory tone that characterizes this epistle; nor the deference it indicates to the wishes and opinions of the parent to whom it was addressed. It was, apparently, written in reply to a previous communication from his mother in relation to the same subject.

We gather from incidental events that many practical objections to the acceptance of the post of Commander-in-Chief of the Virginian Frontier Army, existed at this juncture; and we may infer that the sagacious and far-seeing maternal eye discerned these difficulties, and that Mrs. Washington counselled her son to avoid responsibilities, that existing and uncontrollable circumstances might easily render not only devoid of honor or advantage, but personally unfortunate and injurious.

Thus did this gifted woman, by claims the most irresistible, mature and perpetuate an influence

* Sparks' Life of Washington.

and authority, that remained undiminished and undisputed, when her son had attained the pinnacle of earthly fame.

Before dismissing this portion of our narrative, we cannot refrain from expressing our deep regret at an almost entire want of material for those minute details, which, when they relate to incidents of personal history, serve so much better than mere description, to illustrate character and exhibit the peculiar and individualizing traits which alone can deepen and fill up, so to speak, the faint outline presented in the delineations of the general historian.

CHAPTER III.

He shall not dread Misfortune's angry mien,
Nor feebly sink beneath her tempest rude,
Whose soul hath learn'd, through many a trying scene,
To smile at fate, and suffer unsubdued. METASTASIO.

To solemnize this day, the glorious sun
Stays in his course, and plays the alchemist;
Turning, with splendor of his precious eye,
The meagre, cloddy earth to glittering gold:
The yearly course, that brings this day about,
Shall never see it but a holy day! SHAKSPEARE.

THE events of the disordered times immediately preceding the Revolution, were now rapidly developing. Following each other in startling and fateful succession, and finally resulting in the ever-memorable Declaration of Independence, Mrs. Washington suddenly beheld her son elevated to a position surrounded by dangers the most imminent, and comprehending responsibilities the most solemn and portentous that can devolve upon human agency.

Resting her fears, her aspirations, and her faith, upon that Support which could alone sustain the spirit of so affectionate and so discerning a parent, amid trials thus peculiar and severe, we see this heroic woman resigning herself with the same tranquil submission, and the same unaffected cheerfulness, by which her life had hitherto been distinguished, to the decrees of an overruling and inscrutable Destiny.

Before his departure from his native State, to assume the command of the patriots assembled at Cambridge, the American Commander-in Chief, ever mindful of his Mother's comfort and happiness, even when most burdened by public cares and obligations, assisted in effecting her removal from her country residence in its vicinity, to Fredericksburg.

Mrs. Washington was remunerated for thus renouncing a home hallowed by many tender and time-honored associations, the peaceful asylum of her youthful family in the days of her early bereavement, the scene of their innocent sports, their juvenile education, and of her own strenuous exertions and self-sacrificing devotion during so many years of her life, by being placed in much nearer proximity to her friends and relatives, and in a position more secure from danger than any precaution could have rendered an isolated, rural abode. And as she preferred to maintain an individual establishment, even after her home ceased to be the permanent residence of any of her children, this arrangement was peculiarly suitable and desirable.

Bestowing on him the more than ægis-shield of her blessing and her prayers, the patriotic mother bade adieu to her Son, for a period, the duration and events of which no mortal vision could even faintly discern.

Long familiar with the most effectual means of escape from the dominion of too-anxious thought, she hastened, after this painful parting, to busy herself with the arrangement and care of her new home, and sought in active usefulness and industry, not only the solace of her own "private griefs" and apprehensions, but the high pleasure that springs from the consciousness of doing good.

Ever possessed of far too much genuine self-respect and enlightenment to regard the necessity of homely toil as degrading or unfortunate, her practical ingenuity and personal efforts now supplied, in a good degree, the many deficiencies and deprivations arising from the pressing exigencies of the times, and materially assisted, not only in providing for the wants of her own household, but in furnishing the means of that liberal charity which she had always exercised, however limited her resources, and which was not remitted when increasing occasion had arisen for its continuance.

> "Whoso in pomp of proud estate, quoth she,
> Does swim, and bathes himself in courtly bliss,
> Does waste his daies in dark obscuritie,
> And in oblivion buried is.
> Where ease abounds 'yts eath to doe amis,
> But who his limbs with labor, and his mynd
> Behaves with cares, cannot so easy mis."

Though long past the meridian of life, her equanimity, her healthful habits, and the systematic uniformity of her daily existence, still gave this exemplary matron the physical power essential for carrying into effect her plans of self-dependence and benevolent usefulness.

It was, at this time, her almost daily custom, seated in an old-fashioned, open chaise, to visit her little farm in the vicinity of the town, and while there, to drive about the fields giving directions and personally superintending their execution.

Mrs. Washington is said to have required from

those about her a prompt and literal obedience, somewhat resembling that demanded by proper military subordination ; a habit doubtless arising, in some degree, from a consciousness of the mental power that enabled her rightly to judge, and wisely to direct.

On one occasion, as we are told, she reproved an agent, who, relying upon his own judgment, had disobeyed her orders, saying, "I command you,—there is nothing left for you but to obey!"

Thus, while occupied in her favorite pursuits, and preserved from all sense of loneliness, by the frequent and interesting visits of her children and grand-children, who were invariably most assiduous and affectionate in their endeavors to contribute to her happiness, several years rolled away.

Nor, as may well be supposed, did Mrs. Washington, in the meanwhile, look with an unobservant or unsympathizing eye, upon the changing and momentous aspect of public affairs. Her residence in Fredericksburg enabled her early to obtain the most important intelligence of the day, and we may believe the respectful attention of her Son, speedily and constantly supplied her with information denied to those possessing less claim upon his confidence and regard.

If not always as sanguine of the ultimate triumph of the American arms, as more youthful and ardent spectators of the Revolutionary contest, she watched the progress of national affairs, with patient and tranquil expectation. Frequently raising her thoughtful gaze from the painful contemplation of her country's struggles, towards the Omnipotent Friend who aids the sacred cause of Liberty and Right, she gained a firm and hopeful constancy that shielded her noble spirit, alike from unfounded enthusiasm, and desponding distrust; and that rendered her an example, worthy of all honor, to those mothers, who, like herself, had resigned their sons to their country, in the hour of her greatest need.

When the glorious and heart-warming intelligence of the successful passage of the Delaware,* by Washington and his brave companions in arms, was communicated to his Mother, by the numerous friends who hastened to rejoice with, and to felicitate her upon so auspicious and important an occurrence, she received the tidings with placid self-possession, and expressed her pleasure at the brightening prospects of her native land.

* Dec. 1776.

But in relation to such portions of the despatches of her visitors as contained eulogistic allusions to her Son, she simply remarked, that "George appeared to have deserved well of his country for such signal services," and added :—

"But, my good Sirs, here is too much flattery! —still, George will not forget the lessons I have taught him—he will not forget *himself*, though he is the subject of so much praise."

And when, after the lapse of long, dark years of national gloom and suffering, Mrs. Washington was, at last, informed* of the crowning event of the great conflict—the surrender of Lord Cornwallis, she raised her hands with profound reverence and gratitude towards Heaven, and fervently exclaimed, "Thank God!—war will now be ended, and peace, independence and happiness bless our country!"

An interval of nearly seven perilous and adventurous years had passed, when this illustrious American matron enjoyed the happiness again to behold her victor-crowned and illustrious Son.

Upon the return of the combined armies from Yorktown, the COMMANDER-IN-CHIEF repaired im-

* To whose thoughtful care Mrs. W. owed the *Express* despatched to her with this grateful news, may easily be surmised.

mediately to Fredericksburg, attended by a numerous and splendid suite, composed of the most distinguished European and American officers who had shared his protracted toils and his final triumph.

No sooner had Washington dismounted than he sent a messenger to apprize his Mother of his arrival, with a request to be informed when it would be her pleasure to receive him.

Then, dismissing for a time the attributes and attendants of greatness, he repaired, unaccompanied and on foot, to the modest mansion where his venerable parent awaited his coming.

Mrs. Washington was alone and occupied in some ordinary domestic avocation, when the gladdening intelligence of her Son's approaching visit was communicated to her.

She met him on the threshold with a cordial embrace, her face beaming with unmingled pleasure, and welcomed him by the endearing and well-remembered appellation associated with the pleasing memories of early years.

The quick eye of maternal tenderness readily discerned the furrowed traces of the ceaseless and wearing responsibilities that had for years been the burden of his thoughts, and in the unforgotten tones and with the simple affectionateness of other days, Mrs. Washington immediately and earnestly adverted to the subject of her son's health.

At length, turning the conversation to scenes and themes hallowed to each by the most cherished remembrances, these deeply-attached and happily reunited relatives talked long of mutual friends and former times. But to the peerless fame of the Commander-in-Chief of the Armies of America, *there was not the most remote allusion!*

Yet, as the immortal SAVIOR OF HIS COUNTRY gazed upon the beloved and expressive countenance turned approvingly and affectionately upon him, his happiness was unalloyed and exalted as earth can bestow.

CHAPTER IV.

There fell a moment's thrilling silence round,—
A breathless pause!—the hush of hearts that beat
And limbs that quiver:— HEMANS.

And blessed was her presence there—
Each heart, expanding, grew more gay;
Yet something loftier still than fear,
Kept men's familiar looks away! SCHILLER.

Why then should witless man so much misweene
That nothing is but that which he hath seen. SPENSER.

THE unexpected arrival of WASHINGTON and his Suite, created the most enthusiastic delight among the citizens of Fredericksburg.

Not only the inhabitants of the town, but numbers of gentlemen from its vicinity, hastened to welcome the deliverers of their country with every demonstration of respect and hospitality: happiness irradiated every face, and all were soon engrossed by the eager preparations for festive pleasure.

It was determined to celebrate the joyful occa sion by a splendid Ball.

Mrs. Washington received a special invitation. She answered, that "although her dancing days were *pretty well over*, she should feel happy in contributing to the general festivity."

The company assembled at a much earlier hour than modern fashion would sanction. Gay belles and dignified matrons graced the occasion arrayed in rich laces and bright brocades,—the well-preserved relics of scenes when neither national misfortune nor private calamity forbade their use.

Numerous foreign officers were present, in the brilliant uniforms of their respective corps, glittering with the dazzling insignia of royal favor and successful courage.

Thither came veteran heroes, the blessed and honored of after times, whose war-scathed visages bespoke the unflinching bravery and persevering devotion with which they had served their country, through long years of hardship and danger.

There, too, now swayed only by the light breath of pleasure, waved in billowy folds, the dear-won banners of the "tented field." Music poured its spirit-stirring strains upon the soldier's ear, not to summon him to deeds of arms, but, by its gentler influences, to inspire the chivalrous gallantry that well became the hour,—the gleesome jest, the merry laugh,

"Nods, and becks, and wreathed smiles!"

But despite the soul-soothing charm of music, the fascinations of female loveliness, and the flattering devotion of the gallant brave, all was eager suspense and expectation, until there entered, unannounced and unattended, the MOTHER OF WASHINGTON, leaning on the arm of her SON.

Hushed was each noisy tone, subdued each whispered word, as with quiet dignity and unaffected grace they slowly advanced.

Nature had stamped upon the brow of both, the unmistakable signet of nobility, and

"The vision and the faculty divine"

spoke in the imposing countenance of each, and directed every movement of the majestic pair.

All hastened to approach this august presence; the European officers to be presented to the parent of their beloved Commander, and old friends, neighbors, and acquaintances, to tender the compliments and congratulations appropriate to the occasion.

Mrs. Washington received these peculiar demonstrations of respect and friendship, with perfect self-possession and unassuming courtesy. She wore the simple, but becoming and appropriate costume of the Virginia ladies of the olden time, and even

"The cynosure of beauty's sheen"

was for a time forgotten, while all eyes and all hearts were irresistibly attracted by the winning address and unpretending appearance of the venerable lady.

The European strangers gazed long in wondering amazement, upon this sublime and touching spectacle. Accustomed to the meretricious display of European courts, they regarded with astonishment her unadorned attire, and the mingled simplicity and majesty for which the language and manners of the MOTHER OF WASHINGTON were so remarkable.

They spoke of women renowned in classic lore:—the names of the celebrated Voluminia, and of the noble mother of the Gracchi, broke involuntarily from their lips; and they spontaneously rendered the tribute of admiration and reverence at the shrine of native Dignity and real Worth.

Having, for some time, regarded with serene benignity, the brilliant and festive scene, which she had so amiably consented to honor by her presence, Mrs. Washington expressed the cordial hope that the happiness of all might continue undiminished until the hour of general separation should arrive, and quietly adding, that "it was time for old people to be at home," retired as she had entered, leaning on the arm of the Commander-in-Chief.

Perhaps it will interest some of our lady-readers to know that the immortal WASHINGTON danced on this occasion for the last time;—in the stately minuet, so well adapted to the advantageous display of his graceful air, and elegant and imposing form. He is also described as having been inspired with great cheerfulness and animation, while momentarily courting the aërial graces. The French gentlemen who participated in the pleasures of the evening, protested that Paris itself could boast nothing more perfect than the dancing of the fair and the gallant Americans assembled at this celebrated Ball.

CHAPTER V.

> Her house
> Was ordered well; her children taught the way
> Of life—who, rising up in honor, called
> Her blest.
> *   *   *   *   *   *
> In virtue fair,
> Adorned with modesty, and matron grace
> Unspeakable, and love—her face was like
> The light, most welcome to the eye of man. POLLOK.

> Who sat 'mongst men like a descended god,
> *   *   *   *   *
> Who liv'd in court, which it is rare to do,
> Most praised, most loved:
> A sample to the youngest; to the most mature
> A glass that feated them. SHAKSPEARE.

RE-ESTABLISHED at Mount Vernon, it was the earnest desire of WASHINGTON that his MOTHER should thenceforth reside under his roof.

He had frequently before, urged the same request, and his sister, Mrs. Lewis,* who was always most assiduous in fulfilling the duties im-

* Mrs. Fletcher Lewis, of Fredericksburg, the only sister of Washington, whom she so closely resembled, that when she was arrayed in his usual head-dress, her features were undistinguishable from his.

posed by nature and affection, had repeatedly endeavored to persuade her aged parent to live apart from her no longer.

But the venerable matron, notwithstanding the affectionate entreaties of her children, continued to conduct a separate establishment, with the same indefatigable industry and judicious management which she had earlier exhibited. She still obeyed—

> "The breezy call of incense-breathing morn"

with as much alacrity as of yore, and still gave her attention to the most minute details of domestic affairs.

In this tranquil retreat, where

> "None knew her but to love,
> None named her but to praise,"

she long continued to receive the frequent and fondly-respected visits of her many old and attached friends as well as of her children* and her

* We find many proofs in the published Correspondence of WASHINGTON, of the affectionate devotion with which he paid this tribute of respect to his mother. Thus, he assigns his absence on a visit to her, as a reason for not previously replying to a letter from the Secretary of Congress; and afterwards again, in a letter to Major-General KNOX, he offers the same explanation of a

children's children, blessed in her happy and honored age, by the soothing consciousness of a virtuous and well-spent life.

To the urgent and oft-repeated requests of her children, that she would make with them the home of her age, Mrs. Washington replied:—

"I thank you for your dutiful and affectionate offers, but my wants are few in this life, and I feel perfectly competent to take care of myself."

And when her son-in-law, Colonel Lewis, proposed to assume the general superintendence of her affairs, she resolutely answered—

"Do you, Fielding, keep my books in order, for your eyesight is better than mine, but leave the executive management to me."

Previous to his departure for France, after the termination of the Revolutionary War, the Marquis de La Fayette visited Fredericksburg, expressly for the purpose of making his personal adieus to the mother of his beloved hero-friend, and that he might solemnly invoke her blessing.

similar delay. When his mother was ill, we perceive that he pleads this honorable errand, without reserve, as presenting claims superior to any public obligation. In an epistle written towards the close of the year 1788, we find allusions to a prolonged sojourn under the maternal roof, &c., &c.

This amiable visitor, who had frequently before enjoyed the happiness of conversing with her, repaired to the unobtrusive abode of Mrs. Washington, accompanied by one of her grandsons.

As they approached the house, they observed an aged lady working in the adjoining garden. The materials composing her dress were of home-manufacture, and she wore over her time-silvered hair, a plain straw bonnet.

"There, Sir," said the younger gentleman, "is my grandmother."

Mrs. Washington received her distinguished guest, with great cordiality, and with her usual frank simplicity of address.

"Ah, Marquis!" she exclaimed, "you see an old woman;—but come, I can make you welcome to my poor dwelling, without the parade of changing my dress."

The conversation of this interesting group soon turned, as was most natural, upon the brightening prospects of the young Republic.

The Marquis spoke of the deep interest he cherished in all that related to the prosperity of the land of his adoption, and poured forth the fond and glowing encomiums of a full heart at each allusion to his former Chief,—his friend, his Mentor, his "hero."

To the praises thus enthusiastically lavished upon her son, by the noble Frenchman, his hostess only replied, "*I am not surprised at what George has done, for he was always a good boy.*"

Thus did the true greatness of this extraordinary woman often manifest itself. It was her pleasure frequently to revert to the early days of her august Son, and to express her approbation of his dutiful and upright conduct; but she never appeared in the slightest degree elated by the honors that were showered "thick and fast" upon his glorious name.

With unaffected piety, she referred each and every occurrence of life to the Great First Cause, and when the notes of jubilant praise swelled high, even above the din of battle and the wailings of a nation's despair, it was her earnest maternal aspiration that the "good boy" of her early care, might never "*forget himself!*"

"—— For by the dread decree of Heaven,
Short is the date to earthly grandeur given,
And vain are all attempts to roam beyond
Where fate has fixed the everlasting bound."

Mrs. Washington was always remarkable for that unequivocal proof of superiority, the powerful influence she exerted over the minds of others.

Her ideas of the respect due to her as a parent, remained unchanged either by the lapse of time, or by the development of mighty events, with which her wonderful Son was so closely identified. Ever his trusted counsellor and friend, to her he was always the same in relative position.* To her he owed his existence; to her the early discipline of his extraordinary intellect, and of his high moral nature; and to her he was indebted for the sage advice and prudent guidance of maturer years.

Nor did her son manifest the slightest dissent

* This peculiarity forcibly reminds us of an expressive incident in the life of the mother of the Buonapartes—*Madame Mere.* On one occasion, when the Emperor Napoleon gave audience to the several members of his family, while walking in one of the galleries of the Tuilleries, among his other relatives, his mother advanced towards him. The Emperor extended his hand to her to kiss, as he had done when his brothers and sisters approached him, "No!" said she, "you are the King, the Emperor of all the rest, but you are *my son!*" We leave our readers to draw the contrast irresistibly suggested by this anecdote, between the Republican Statesman and the Emperor of all the French.

from this sentiment. We are informed by one* well entitled to be regarded as unquestionable authority, that "to the last moments of his venerable parent he yielded to her will the most implicit obedience, and felt for her person and character the highest respect and the most enthusiastic attachment."

Perhaps the life of this celebrated lady afforded no more convincing proof of the genuine nobleness of her character, than was evinced by the constancy with which she maintained the peculiar sentiments and principles of her youth. We may believe that a mind less perfectly balanced, would have rendered, at least, an unconscious homage to the power of circumstances so novel and so imposing as those in which she was placed.

It was Mrs. Washington's habit, during the latter years of her life, to repair daily to a secluded spot near her dwelling, formed by overhanging rocks and trees. There, isolated from worldly thoughts and objects, she sought in devout prayer and meditation, most appropriate preparation for

* G. W. P. Custis, Esq., the grandson of Mrs. Martha Washington, to whose interesting "Recollections" we are indebted for most of the particulars relative to the life of Mrs. W., now in the possession of the literary public.

the great change which she was admonished by her advanced age, might nearly await her.

But one of the many weaknesses that usually characterize humanity, was manifested by this heroic woman. Upon the approach of a thunder-storm she invariably retired to her own apartment, and remained there until calmness was restored to the elements. This almost constitutional timidity, was occasioned by a singularly distressing incident of her youth—the instant death, from the effects of lightning, of a young friend, who was, at the moment when the accident occurred, sitting close beside her.

The appearance of Mrs. Washington is said to have been pleasing. Her countenance was agreeable and highly expressive, and her person well-proportioned and of average height.

CHAPTER VI.

She goes unto the Rock sublime
Where halts above the Eternal Sea, the shuddering
Child of time! SCHILLER.

BEFORE WASHINGTON'S departure for the seat of government, to assume the duties of President of the United States, he went to Fredericksburg to pay his parting respects to his aged mother.

Mrs. Washington's health had now become so infirm as to impress her with the conviction that she beheld for the last time the crowning blessing of her declining age.

Forgetting all else in the same mournful belief, the calm self-possession that no calamity had for years been able to shake, yielded to the claims of nature, and, overpowered by painful emotion, the mighty chieftain wept long, with bowed head, over the wasted form of his revered and much-loved parent.

Sustained, even in this trying hour, by her native strength of mind, the heroic Mother fervently invoked the blessing of Heaven upon her sorrowing Son, and solemnly bestowing her own, bade him pursue the path in which public duty summoned him to depart.

Mrs. Washington retained unimpaired possession of her mental faculties to her latest moments, but during the last three years of her life, her physical powers were much diminished by the effects of the distressing malady with which she was long afflicted.

This painful disease* terminated her earthly existence in her eighty-third year. Her death occurred on the 25th of August, 1789. She had been forty-six years a widow.

The last hours of this incomparable woman were accompanied by a tranquillity and resignation most unlike the usual death-bed attendants of the world's scathed devotees.

An extract from a letter written by WASHINGTON to his sister, soon after the decease of their Mother, will best illustrate the methodical calmness with which she made a final adjustment of her temporal affairs. Our readers will also, thus become possessed of the minutest information in relation to the concluding scenes of Mrs. Wash-

* Cancer in the breast.

ington's life, that persevering research has enabled us to discover.

"To Mrs. Betty Lewis.

"New York, 13th September, 1789.

"My Dear Sister:—

* * * * * *

"Awful and affecting as the death of a parent is, there is consolation in knowing that Heaven has spared ours to an age beyond which few attain, and favored her with the full enjoyment of her faculties and as much bodily strength as usually falls to the lot of fourscore. Under these considerations, and a hope that she is translated to a happier place, it is the duty of her relatives to yield due submission to the decrees of the Creator. When I was last at Fredericksburg, I took a final leave of my mother, never expecting to see her more.

"It will be impossible for me at this distance, and circumstanced as I am, to give the smallest attention to the execution of her will; nor, indeed is much required, if, as she directs, no security should be given, nor appraisement made of her estate; but that the same should be allotted to the devisees with as little trouble and delay as may be. How far this is legal I know not. Mr.

Merced can, and I have no doubt would, advise you if asked, which I wish you to do. If the ceremony of inventorying, appraising, &c., can be dispensed with, all the rest, as the will declares that few or no debts are owing, can be done with very little trouble. Every person may, in that case, immediately receive what is specially devised.

"Were it not that the specific legacies, which are given to me by the will, are meant and ought to be considered and received as mementoes of paternal affection in the last solemn act of life, I should not be desirous of receiving or removing them; but in this point of view, I set a value on them much beyond their intrinsic worth."

We are, of course, indebted to Mr. Sparks' LIFE OF WASHINGTON for the communication from which this extract is derived. We also give Mrs. Washington's age, at the time of her death, as stated by Mr. S., though it is sometimes represented to have been still more advanced.

We cannot better, or more suitably, close this chapter than by presenting our readers with the just, discriminating, and graceful eulogy expressed in the following eloquent passage from the pen of the same accurate and accomplished author:—

"The weighty charge of five young children, the eldest of whom was eleven years old, the superintendence of their education, and the management of complicated affairs, demanded no common share of resolution, resource of mind, and strength of character. In these important duties, Mrs. Washington acquitted herself with great fidelity to her trust, and with entire success. Her good sense, assiduity, tenderness, and vigilance overcame every obstacle; and as the richest reward of a mother's solicitude and toil, she had the happiness to see all her children come forward with a fair promise into life, filling the sphere allotted to them in a manner equally honorable to themselves, and to the parent who had been the only guide of their principles, conduct, and habits. She lived to witness the noble career of her eldest son, till by his own rare merits, he was raised to the head of a nation, and applauded and revered by the whole world. It has been said, that there never was a great man, the elements of whose greatness might not be traced to the original characteristics or early influence of his mother. If this be true, how much do mankind owe to the mother of Washington."

CHAPTER VII.

Thou high-born spirit, on whose countenance,
Pure and beloved, is seen reflected all
That Heaven and Nature can on earth achieve!—

MICHEL ANGELO.

"There sounds not to the trump of Fame,
The echo of a noble name!"

As well might we assimilate the airy graces of a modern belle, arrayed in the ample costume of the present day, with the undraped proportions and severe beauty of an antique statue, as to compare the life and character of the MOTHER OF WASHINGTON with those of the women of our own times, or adjudge her attire, character, and manners by the arbitrary rules of fashionable conventionalism!

Hers was a character that might stand forth in its natural majesty, unrelieved by the "aids and appliances" of adventitious circumstance; and the grateful reverence which we instinctively accord her, can only be inspired by transcendent worth.

Those who best knew her inestimable qualities, earnestly strive to impress us with the conviction that she was gifted with attributes adapting her in a most extraordinary degree to the immortal part assigned her in the drama of human existence. Yet the stern virtues that served to mould a future Hero, were attempered by womanly tenderness and sympathy; and we associate them in our remembrance with the practical kindness and unostentatious habits that equally marked her daily life.

The philosophy so forcibly illustrated in the history of Mary Washington is not that of Plato, of Socrates, or of Zeno, but that of CHRIST!

Her equanimity was not the result of constitutional insensibility, nor yet of a debasing stoicism, but of the dominant influence of immutable *Religious Principle,* forever supreme, alike over the weaknesses of nature and the promptings of worldly ambition.

The life and character of this illustrious matron, in some points of general resemblance, reminded us of those of the self-devoted Scottish Covenanters of old: like them, she regarded with indifference, if not with contempt, the inconvenient requisitions of ceremony and the unscrupulous exactions of corrupting fashion; like them she sought to obtain from the Bible alone her invariable rule of life; and like them, she worshipped God surrounded by the majestic companionship of nature,

> "Not 'neath the domes, where crumbling arch and column
> Attest the feebleness of mortal hand;
> But in that fane, most catholic and solemn,
> Which God has plann'd!"

Her Name and her Fame are the priceless inheritance, not of her native country alone, but of every land that boasts a knowledge of the glorious achievements of the immortal *Champion of Liberty!*

Her name will be revered, and her memory cherished, when those of mighty empires and world-renowned sovereigns shall have sunk forever into the whirlpool of Oblivion: unsullied, unobscured by the supremacy of power and the lapse of ages, they will beam forth resplendent in the sanctified lustre of MORAL GRANDEUR.

At the feet of the proud daughter of the Ptolemies, the conquerors of the world laid down their crowns, yet Clio, faithful to the truth, withholds the meed of honor from the coward soul that could not brave adversity. The history of Christina, the royal Swedish wanderer, scarce serves, at best, to "point a moral," and awakens no more exalted sentiment than one of pitying regret. Maria Theresa, despite her many and exalted excellencies, sacrificed some of woman's first, best duties on the altar of ambition. And who will demand either love or veneration for the memory of England's greatest Queen, renowned as much for her most unfeminine faults, as for her boasted masculine virtues.

Imagination may pall in the contemplation of mere charms of person,—even though unrivalled,—when associated with the moral cowardice of the famous Egyptian Queen; we may regard profound erudition without respect, when allied with the undisciplined instincts and uncontrolled passions of the celebrated daughter of the Great Gustavus; or hear with indifference, tributes to the religious enthusiasm and regal heroism of the Empress-King;* or turn with unsympathizing dislike from the haughty, indomitable, relentless Elizabeth; but when shall the daughters of Co-

* "BEHOLD OUR KING!" was the enthusiastic exclamation of the brave Hungarian nobles, at the most touching and sublime moment of the life of this great sovereign.

lumbia be weary of imbibing the benign and hallowed influences inseparably associated with the pure and sacred name of MARY WASHINGTON?

The combined qualities of her consistent, elevated, conscience-illuminated character, constitute a *perfect whole,* that most beautifully and strikingly illustrates alike the *Woman* and the *Christian,* in the highest and most comprehensive sense of those expressive words.

Enshrined in the *Sanctuary of Home,* her sublime example is the peerless boast of her country; and it shall but brighten as it recedes with revolving years.

Radiant in the zenith of Columbia's Heaven, beams the star of her fame, fixed and enduring as

"—— the cerulean arch we see,
MAJESTIC IN ITS OWN SIMPLICITY!"

CHAPTER VIII.

"There are deeds which should not pass away,
And names that must not wither, though the earth
Forgets her empires with a just decay,
The enslavers and the enslaved, their death and birth."

Act!—for in action are wisdom and glory;
Fame, immortality, these are its crown;
Wouldst thou illumine the tablets of story,
Build on achievements thy doom of renown.
Honor and feeling are given to cherish;
Cherish them, then, though all else should decay;
Landmarks be these that are never to perish,
Stars that will shine on the duskiest day. J. G. Von Salis.

The remains of Mrs. Washington were interred at Fredericksburg, in Virginia, where she so long resided, and where she remained till the time of her death.

For many years after her decease her place of sepulchre was undistinguished by any mark of public respect; but more recently a tasteful and splendid monument has been erected to the memory of Mrs. Washington, under the direction of a Committee representing the citizens of her native State.*

* In preparing these pages for the press, the author, having

The ceremony of laying the corner-stone of this highly appropriate mausoleum, was performed by Andrew Jackson, who was at the time President of the United States, and who was, therefore, very properly invited by the Monumental Committee to assume that honorary task.

This interesting celebration occurred on the seventh of May, 1833.

General Jackson went from the seat of government to Fredericksburg, attended by the several members of the National Cabinet and by a numerous concourse of highly respectable citizens and strangers. The inhabitants of Fredericksburg, also united in great numbers, with this imposing assemblage; and the whole scene was characterized by the most cordial and respectful interest, and by deep pathos and solemnity.

The President distinguished the occasion by an

not the slightest reason to suspect their accuracy, assumed as facts the statements in relation to this public monument contained in "KNAPP'S FEMALE BIOGRAPHY." Truth, however, compels her, most reluctantly, to admit that, after the MS. was delivered to the Publisher, a newspaper article, purporting to be written at Fredericksburg, met her eye, in which it was asserted that the tomb of Mrs. Washington has not been completed, and that it, at present, exhibits painful indications of neglect and decay.

elegant eulogistic Address, from which we present our readers with a few paragraphs.

* * * * *

"We are assembled, fellow-citizens, to witness and assist in an interesting ceremony. More than a century has passed away since she to whom this tribute of respect is about to be paid, entered upon the active scenes of life. A century fertile in wonderful events, and of distinguished men who have participated in them. Of these our country has furnished a full share; and of these distinguished men she has produced a WASHINGTON! If he was "first in war, first in peace, first in the hearts of his countrymen," we may say, without the imputation of national vanity, that if not the first, he was in the very first rank of those, too few indeed, upon whose career mankind can look back without regret, and whose memory and example will furnish themes of eulogy for the patriot, wherever free institutions are honored and maintained. His was no false glory, deriving its lustre from the glare of splendid and destructive actions, commencing in professions of attachment to his country, and terminating in the subversion of her freedom. Far different is the radiance which surrounds his name and fame.

It shines mildly and equally, and guides the philanthropist and citizen in the path of duty; and it will guide them long after those false lights which have attracted too much attention, shall have been extinguished in darkness.

"In the grave before us, lie the remains of his Mother. Long has it been unmarked by any monumental tablet, but not unhonored. You have undertaken the pious duty of erecting a column to her name, and of inscribing upon it, the simple but affecting words, "Mary, the Mother of Washington." No eulogy could be higher, and it appeals to the heart of every American.

"These memorials of affection and gratitude, are consecrated by the practice of all ages and nations. They are tributes of respect to the dead, but they convey practical lessons of virtue and wisdom to the living. The mother and son are beyond the reach of human applause; but the bright example of paternal and filial excellence, which their conduct furnishes cannot but produce the most salutary effects upon our countrymen. Let their example be before us from the first lesson which is taught the child, till the mother's duties yield to the course of preparation and action which nature prescribes for him.

* * * * *

"Tradition says, that the character of Washington was strengthened, if not formed, by the care and precepts of his mother. She was remarkable for the vigor of her intellect and the firmness of her resolution.

* * * * *

"In tracing the few recollections which can be gathered, of her principles and conduct, it is impossible to avoid the conviction, that these were closely interwoven with the destiny of her son. The great points of his character are before the world. He who runs may read them in his whole career, as a citizen, a soldier, a magistrate. He possessed unerring judgment, if that term can be applied to human nature; great probity of purpose, high moral principles, perfect self-possession, untiring application, and inquiring mind, seeking information from every quarter, and arriving at its conclusions with a full knowledge of the subject; and he added to these an inflexibility of resolution, which nothing could change but a conviction of error. Look back at the life and conduct of his mother, and at her domestic government, as they have this day been delineated by the Chairman of the Monumental Committee, and as they were known to her contemporaries, and have been described by them, and they will be found admirably adapted to form and develop, the elements of such a character. The power of greatness was there; but had it not been guided and directed by maternal solicitude and judgment, its possessor, instead of presenting to the world, examples of virtue, patriotism and wisdom, which will be precious in all succeeding ages, might have added to the number of those master-spirits, whose fame rests upon the faculties they have abused, and the injuries they have committed.

* * * * *

"Fellow-citizens, at your request, and in your name, I now deposit this plate in the spot destined for it; and when the American pilgrim shall, in after ages, come up to this high and holy place, and lay his hand upon this sacred column, may he recall the virtues of her, who sleeps beneath, and depart with his affections purified, and his piety strengthened, while he invokes blessings upon the Mother of Washington."

The following impressive lines were prepared for this interesting ceremonial, by our gifted countrywoman, Mrs. L. H. Sigourney:

"Long hast thou slept unnoted. Nature stole
In her soft ministry, around thy bed,
And spread her vernal coverings, violet-gemm'd,
And pearl'd with dews. She bade bright Summer bring
Gifts of frankincense, with sweet song of birds,
And Autumn cast his yellow coronet
Down at thy feet, and stormy Winter speak
Hoarsely of man's neglect. But now we come
To do thee homage, Mother of our Chief,
Fit homage, such as honoreth him who pays!
Methinks we see thee, as in olden time,
Simple in garb—majestic and serene—
Unaw'd by "pomp and circumstance"—in truth
Inflexible—and with Spartan zeal
Repressing vice, and making folly grave.
Thou didst not deem it woman's part to waste
Life in inglorious sloth, to sport awhile
Amid the flowers, or on the summer wave,
Then fleet like the ephemeron away,
Building no temple in her children's hearts,
Save to the vanity and pride of life
Which she had worshipp'd.

"Of the might that cloth'd
The "Pater Patriæ"—of the deeds that won
A nation's liberty, and earth's applause,
Making Mount Vernon's tomb a Mecca haunt—
For patriot and for sage, while time shall last,
What part was thine, what thanks to thee are due,
Who mid his elements of being wrought
With no uncertain aim—nursing the germs

Of godlike virtue in his infant mind,
We know not,—heaven can tell!

"Rise, noble pile!
And show a race unborn, who rests below—
And say to mothers, what a holy charge
Is theirs—with what a kingly power their love
Might rule the fountains of the new-born mind—
Warn them to wake at early dawn, and sow
Good seed before the world doth sow its tares,
Nor in their toil decline—that angel bands
May put the sickle in, and reap for God,
And gather to his garner.

"Ye who stand
With thrilling breast and kindling cheek this morn,
Viewing the tribute that Virginia pays
To the blest Mother of her glorious Chief;
Ye, whose last thought upon your nightly couch,
Whose first, at waking, is, your cradled son,
What though no dazzling hope aspires to rear
A second Washington, or leave your name,
Wrought out in marble, with your country's tears
Of deathless gratitude,—yet may ye raise
A monument above the stars, a soul
Led by your teachings, and your prayers, to God."

The exquisite taste and perfect keeping, exhibited in this mausoleum, render it one of the most elegant works of art, of which our country boasts. The form is pyramidal; and the height of the obelisk, forty-five feet. The shaft is adorned by a colossal bust of the immortal Washington, and surmounted by the American Eagle, sustaining a civic crown above the heroic head.

Language can scarcely afford a more irresistibly touching illustration of the *moral sublime*, than is contained in the brief sentence inscribed upon this hallowed tomb :—

MARY

THE MOTHER OF

WASHINGTON.

APPENDIX TO MARY WASHINGTON.

APPENDIX TO MARY WASHINGTON.

NOTE A.—"In the year 1538, the Manor of Sulgrave, in Northumberlandshire, was granted to Lawrence Washington, of Gray's Inn, and for some time Mayor of Northampton. He was probably born at Warton, in Lancashire, where his father lived. The grandson of this first proprietor of Sulgrave, who was of the same name, had many children, two of whom, that is, John and Lawrence Washington, being the second and fourth sons, emigrated to Virginia about the year 1657, and settled at Bridge's Creek, on the Potomac River, in the county of Westmoreland The eldest brother, Sir William Washington, married a half-sister of George Villiers, Duke of Buckingham. Lawrence had been a student at Oxford. John had resided on an estate at South Cave, in Yorkshire, which give rise to an erroneous tradition among his descendants, that their ancestor came from the North of England. The two brothers bought lands in Virginia, and became successful planters.

"John Washington, not long after coming to America, was employed in a military command against the Indians, and rose to the rank of Colonel. The parish in which he lived was also named after him. He married Anne Pope, by whom he had two sons, Lawrence and John, and a daughter. The elder son, Lawrence, married Mildred Warner, of Gloucester County, and had three children, John, Augustine, and Mildred."

"Augustine Washington, the second son, was twice married. His first wife was Jane Butler, by whom he had three sons and a daughter; Butler, who died in infancy, Lawrence, Augustine, and Jane, the last of whom died likewise, when a child." His second wife was Mary Ball

SPARKS' LIFE OF WASHINGTON.

MARTHA WASHINGTON.

MEMOIR

OF

MARTHA WASHINGTON.

A Perfect Woman, nobly planned,
To warn, to comfort, and command;
And yet a spirit, still and bright,
With something of an Angel's light!

Wordsworth.

Not enjoyment, and not sorrow,
Is our destined end or way;
But to act that each to-morrow,
Finds us farther than to-day.

Longfellow.

CONTENTS

OF THE

LIFE OF MARTHA WASHINGTON.

CHAPTER I.

CHAPTER II.

CHAPTER III.

CHAPTER IV.

CHAPTER V.

CHAPTER VI.

CHAPTER VII.

CHAPTER VIII.

CHAPTER IX.

CHAPTER X.

THE WIFE OF WASHINGTON.

CHAPTER I.

Grace was in all her steps, heaven in her eye,
In every gesture, dignity and love. MILTON.

Our youthful summer oft we see
Dance by on wings of game and glee,
Whilst the dark storm resumes its rage.
* * * * *
And such a lot, my theme, was thine,
When thou, of late, wert doom'd to twine,—
Just when the bridal wreath was by,—
The cypress with the myrtle tie. SCOTT.

THE ILLUSTRIOUS SUBJECT of the following Memoir, is first presented to our attention in the interesting position of a youthful *belle* at the Court of the stately representative of British power and rule, within the limits of the proud, aristocratical and wealthy "Old Dominion."

The charms of an agreeable person and a lovely face, enhanced by the superior fascination of winning manners and an amiable disposition combined to render this fair representative of an ancient race, one of the most admired and beloved of the many living flowers assembled during the season of fashion, to grace the Colonial Court of Governor Dinwiddie.

MARTHA DANDRIDGE was born in the County of New Kent, in the Colony of Virginia, in May, 1732. The long line of ancestors from whom she was descended, was originally represented in the Colony by the Rev. Orlando Jones, a Welsh gentleman, who early established himself on the banks of the Potomac.

Miss Dandridge possessed only such artificial accomplishments as the system of domestic instruction, then the sole means of female education in her native land, enabled her to acquire. But she was, happily, endowed by nature, with infinitely more essential qualifications for usefulness and happiness than these could supply—self-respect, good sense, gentleness of temper, a quick perception of propriety, and a ready power of self-adaptation to the exigencies and necessities of practical life.

Though the celebrity early acquired, and the distinguished associations as early commenced by Miss Dandridge, were perpetuated through the accumulated years of a long and varied life, her career in the dazzling realms of fashion, was destined to be as evanescent as it was brilliant and agreeable.

Won by the almost resistless power of a deep and discriminating attachment,—that most exquisitely delicate and expressive of compliments,—at the age of seventeen, before adulation and her unusual *succès de société* had alloyed the ingenuous simplicity, or diminished the buoyant enthusiasm of her noble nature,

> "——— in the lustre of her youth, she gave
> Her hand, with her heart in it, to"—

one of her numerous admirers, Colonel Daniel Parke Custis, a son of the Hon. John Custis of Arlington.

Through her eventful life, it was the happy fate of this distinguished lady to be the *object of warm and disinterested affection;* and this characteristic of her history was eminently illustrated by the attachment of Col. Custis, who, in opposition to the more ambitious matrimonial designs of his father,—himself a King's Counsellor, and desirous of public honors for his son,—preferred the young and lovely MISS DANDRIDGE to all the allurements of political distinction and unbounded wealth.

The consent of the reluctant and ambitious King's Counsellor yielded, at last, to the firmness and ardor of manly constancy, the successful lover triumphantly bore away his fair prize, to his plantation in her native County of Kent.

The residence of Col. Custis was situated on the shore of the Pamunkey River, and was known by the now peculiarly significant appellation of the "*White House.*"

He was a highly prosperous planter, and a pleasing impersonation of the Virginia gentleman of the olden time. Possessed of sterling integrity, and eminently gifted with the refined and elevated sentiments so agreeably illustrated by the peculiar incidents connected with his matrimonial engagement, he was, also, endowed by nature with a heart as generously liberal as his purse was ample and overflowing. Living in times when hospitality was not only practised as a duty and a virtue, but regarded as affording some of the most innocent and delightful gratifications of domestic life, his bountiful board was habitually spread, like those of the feudal lords of other days and other lands, not alone for numerous vassals and dependants, but in preparation for the cordial welcome equally awaiting the passing stranger and the expected friend.

The obligations and responsibilities appertaining to the mistress of so extensive an establishment as that of the " White House," however agreeable in their nature, were necessarily, by no means either nominal or light. But she who had voluntarily and "nothing loath," so early exchanged her youthful pleasures and her maiden freedom for the cares and duties of an *American Matron,* readily and cheerfully assimilated herself to her new position.

And when the more interesting and important avocations of a mother were added to those of the wife of a Virginia country gentleman, the home in which Mrs. Custis presided continued to illustrate the judicious system of household arrangement, the wise economy, order, and regularity for which she was through life so remarkable.

To the friends whom she had known and loved in her girlhood, and who still continued to evince undiminished their former interest and regard, time only added nearer ties and more endearing associations, and

> " The wife, the mother, dearer than the bride,"

the sweet home-virtues long went hand in hand with Health, Peace, and Content,—the lovely graces of the fireside!

Thus, for some time, the halcyon days of the domestic felicity of Mrs. Custis glided uninterruptedly on.

But never does earthly happiness continue unalloyed! Death entered, and desolated this Eden of Delight!

The first victim of the destroyer was the hope and joy of his parents,—their eldest child,—whose unusual mental developments gave only too delusive and fleeting promise of the future.

Soon after this melancholy event, Col. Custis (his malady incurably heightened by the effects of overwhelming grief for the loss of his son,) sunk, prematurely, into the grave, when he had scarcely attained the prime of manhood!

With the painfully-touching proof of extraordinary sensibility afforded by the mournful cause of his early death, family tradition unites an anecdote illustrative of another prominent trait in the interesting character of Col. Custis:—"It is related of this amiable gentleman," says his brief biographer and immediate descendant, "that, when on his death-bed, he sent for a tenant, to whom, in settling an account, he was due one shilling. The tenant begged that the Colonel, who had ever been most kind to his tenantry, would not trouble himself at all about such a trifle, as he, the tenant, had forgotten it long ago. "But I have not," rejoined the just and conscientious landlord, and bidding his creditor take up the coin, which had been purposely placed on his pillow, exclaimed, "Now my accounts are all closed with this world!" and shortly after expired.

Thus suddenly deprived, not only of the child whose existence had first awakened in her bosom the holy love and the lofty aspirations of a mother, but, of the friend and counsellor whose changeless affection had long made the sunshine of her life, and upon whom she had so implicitly relied for effective aid in the fulfilment of her solemn and momentous maternal duties, Mrs. Custis did not weakly abandon herself to useless lamentation, or helpless despair. Two children still survived to claim her care and affection; and, after the first burst of impassioned and overpowering sorrow,—seeking strength for the effort where alone it could be found, in the promised aid of a chastening, but merciful Redeemer,—

she nerved herself for conscientious and persevering attention to duties and interests so painfully augmented and so mournfully and deeply important.

Col. Custis gave the highest proof that the romantic attachment and well-founded respect of early days remained undiminished through the lapse of years, by leaving to his widow the exclusive management and disposition, not only of her own pecuniary interests, but of those of her children.

How triumphantly Mrs. Custis proved her ability for the task thus delegated to her, will be best told in the words of the same authority to which we have before referred.—"Independently of extensive and valuable landed estates, the Colonel left thirty thousand* pounds sterling in money, with half that amount to his only daughter Martha. * * * * *

"Mrs. Custis, as sole executrix, managed the

* Mr. Sparks states this sum to have been still larger. He says:—"Mr. Custis had left large landed estates in New Kent County, and forty-five thousand pounds sterling in money. One third part of this property she [Mrs. Custis,] held in her own right, the other two thirds being equally divided between her children."—*Sparks' Life of Washington*, vol. i, p. 105.

extensive landed and pecuniary concerns of the estates with surprising ability, making loans on mortgage, of moneys, and, through her stewards and agents, conducting the sales or exportation of the crops to the best possible advantage."

If not as lightly and blissfully as of old, still peacefully and hopefully, time passed with the widowed mother, while engaged in these needful occupations, and in the most affectionate devotion to the education and happiness of her children, whom it was her sedulous endeavor to inspire with a wish to emulate the virtues of their father ;—thus rendering just homage to his memory, and suitably entitling them to the splendid worldly endowments and to the honorable name which were alike their proud inheritance.

CHAPTER II.

O, young Lochinvar is come out of the West,
Through all the wide Border his steed was the best;
And save his good broadsword, he weapons had none,
He rode all unarm'd, and he rode all alone.
So faithful in love, and so dauntless in war,
There never was knight like the young Lochinvar! SCOTT.

And bright
The lamps shone o'er fair women and brave men:
A thousand hearts beat happily; and when
Music arose with its voluptuous swell,
Soft eyes look'd love to eyes which spake again! BYRON.

BEAUTIFUL, gifted, with great fascination of manner, unusually accomplished, extremely wealthy, youthful, and

"Without any control, but the sweet one of gracefulness,"

it is not surprising,—the usual period of mourning and seclusion passed,—that the hand of MRS. CUSTIS was sought by many and ardent suitors.

The "White House" became again the chosen abode of refined and graceful hospitality, and its fair and gentle mistress once more assumed her place in the elegant and distinguished circle, to the attractions of which her presence had formerly made so agreeable an addition.

But though participating with subdued cheerfulness in the rational enjoyments of social life, and extending equal courtesy to all who came within the sphere of her magic influence; yet a taste, refined, it might be even to fastidiousness, by prolonged and intimate association with one of the most amiable and honorable of men, was not easily satisfied. Nor would the heart that had been so entirely his, through many happy years of wedded love, readily yield itself to the keeping of another.

" Oft she rejects, but never once offends."

Content in her singular freedom from authoritative restraint, conscious of her ability to conduct, unaided, her own business affairs, and those of her children,—young, lovely, admired, respected,—why should she exchange her felicitous independence for a protection, in her peculiar circumstances little better than nominal perchance, or, at least, for many reasons, undesirable and unnecessary? The well-remembered virtues of his father would be the best guide of her son, and her ceaseless assiduity would obtain both for him and for his sister, every advantage that unlimited pecuniary resources and the most affectionate interest could unitedly secure. Why, then, either for their benefit, or for her own happiness, should their mother renounce her present name?

Governed by these numerous, weighty, and seemingly-conclusive reasons, the beautiful widow remained immovably relentless, while each enamored lover pressed, in turn, his glowing and disinterested suit! Eloquence did not shake her resolution, manly beauty and intelligence, polished manners, high honor,—all were vain to ruffle the "waveless calm" of the unresponding heart, in whose peaceful depths lay enshrined—*the treasures of memory!*

At length, by accident, there crossed her path, one, whose Star of Fame was already far in the ascendant in his native State; a patriotic and distinguished citizen-soldier, who could tell

"of most disastrous chances,
Of moving accidents by flood and field,
Of hair-breadth 'scapes i' the imminent deadly breach,
Of being taken by the insolent foe!"*

* Our readers will consider the application of this last line as scarcely involving a *poetic license*, when they recollect the fact recorded in the annexed passage:—

His conversation, his manners, his appearance, combined to prove this interesting stranger no common mortal, no ordinary wooer! Nature had stamped upon his powerful frame and majestic countenance an unmistakable impress of the mental power that dwelt within, and sealed his august brow, with

"The stamp of Fate and fiat of a God!"

Again and again the fascinated soldier sought the presence of the enchanting widow. Again and again he spontaneously acknowledged the winning power of her lithe and graceful form, her bright, expressive face, and the far more potent magic of her *suave* and benignant manners, her noble and disciplined intellect. And he, the victor-crowned,—now himself subdued,—awaited his fate at the hand of the resistless charmer!

What wonder, then, that the lofty resolve to preserve unchanged her womanly liberty, which was erst the high prerogative of MRS. CUSTIS,

Lieutenant Col. Washington, "being joined soon after by the residue of the regiment, and a few other troops, making an aggregate of somewhat less than four hundred men, they erected a small stockade fort; here he was attacked by twelve hundred French and Indians, and after a brave resistance from ten in the morning until night, he capitulated."

NATIONAL PORTRAIT GALLERY.

should, gradually, "melt into thin air," like the scrolled snow-wreath, beneath the ardent gaze of advancing Phœbus!—

> "—— Airy messengers had sought,
> The rosy realms of Fancy through,"

and, with one accord, they yielded the palm of highest merit to the youthful *Washington!*

The favorite charger of the Hero of Monongahela, and his faithful Bishop,* in obedience to the high behest of their noble master, now often traced with him, the familiar way that conducted to the hospitable "White House." Long and often did the impatient war-steed await his time-unheeding rider; long and often did the assiduous attendant marvel at a forgetfulness of commands that on other occasions, sometimes anticipated even his prompt and exact punctuality.

And now, all was in elegant and tasteful preparation in the "White House," for the elaborate and splendid celebration of the approaching bridal.

Numerous relatives and valued friends, aristocratic magnates of the "Old Dominion," stately

* Each bequeathed him by the dying Braddock on the ill-starred field of his last battle.

matrons, and dignified statesmen, the young, the beautiful, the brave, were assembled in honor of nuptials so signally auspicious, so brilliant and so felicitous.

"Much hath the biographer* heard of that marriage, from gray-haired domestics, who waited at the board where love made the feast and WASHINGTON was the guest. And rare and high was the revelry, at that palmy period of Virginia's festal age; for many were gathered at that marriage of the good, the great, the gifted and the gay, while Virginia, with joyous acclamation, hailed in her youthful hero a prosperous and happy bridegroom."

Imagination will better picture the pomp and splendor of this interesting scene than any description of ours. Thus will our readers satisfactorily behold the fairest of Virginia's fair daughters, arrayed in the superb brocades, the costly laces, and sparkling jewels that the Old World alone could then supply; gallant cavaliers, in the elaborate and elegant costumes of the time; the brilliant apartments, the bountiful board, glittering with massive plate, and loaded with sub-

* We borrow the expressive language of the interesting annalist to whose authority we before referred.

stantial viands, rich wines, and delicate conserves. Thus aided they may listen to the gay conversation, the merry song, the whispered words, the blithesome laugh, the flashing wit, the inspiring music, each well befitting the occasion; and watch

"—— the docile footstep to the heave of the sweet measure,
As music wafts the form aloft at its melodious pleasure,
Now breaking through the woven chain of the entangled dance!"

The same magic power will most successfully portray the grace, the loveliness, the tearful smiles, the glowing cheek of the Bride, when warm words and softened looks bespoke the cordial aspirations for her future happiness that swelled the hearts of her friends; and the animated countenance, the majestic mien, the undisguised rapture of the triumphant and love-crowned Soldier.

CHAPTER III.

For still where the firm * * * * *
And the stern, in sweet marriage is blent with the meek,
Rings the concord harmonious, both tender and strong;
* * * * * *
The heart to the heart flows in one, love delighted. SCHILLER.

---

* * Woe to thy dream of delight;
In darkness dissolves the gay frost-work of bliss;
Where now is the picture that Fancy touch'd bright?
W. W. DIMOND.

But lo! a Congress! What, that hallow'd name
Which freed the Atlantic? BYRON.

SOON after their union, which occurred, it is believed, in January, 1759, COLONEL and MRS. WASHINGTON removed from the "White House" to *Mount Vernon,* which continued thenceforth, to be the permanent family residence.*

* Mount Vernon is in Fairfax Co., Virginia. It is pleasantly situated on the south bank of the Potomac, nine miles below Alexandria and fifteen miles from Washington. It may interest some of our readers to learn the *origin of the name* of a spot now possessing so much celebrity. George Washington inherited this residence from his eldest brother, Lawrence, who

The mansion then bearing this name, was much smaller than it afterwards became. It consisted only of the centre of the present building, with but four rooms on the first floor. Its owner had resided there for some years previous to his marriage, but Mount Vernon was now, for the first time, graced by the presence of *a mistress.*

We find many proofs, in his published papers and Correspondence, of the efforts made by Col. Washington to augment the comforts and multiply the embellishments of his home, after it received the fair and gentle inmate, whose happiness was, thenceforth, to be his peculiar care.

Nor was his attention confined to matters appertaining merely to daily convenience, or general improvement,—it extended to all that could lend attractiveness to *home-life*, for the enjoyments of which the inhabitants of Mount Vernon mutually possessed an ardent love.

"held a Captain's commission in the Provincial troops, employed in the celebrated attack against Carthagena, under *Admiral Vernon.* On his return, he settled on his patrimonial estate; which, through respect to his Admiral, he called Mount Vernon." This gentleman died not long afterwards, bequeathing his estate to his only child, in case of whose death it was to descend to his brother George, "with the reservation of the use of the same to the wife during her lifetime."

The following Memoranda of articles to be ordered from Europe, the originals of which were found by Mr. Sparks among Washington's papers, in his own hand-writing, will serve as passing indications of the refined and elegant taste that directed everything within the precincts of the new abode of Mrs. Washington:—

"DIRECTIONS FOR THE BUSTS.—One of Alexander the Great; another of Julius Cæsar; another of Charles XII. of Sweden; and a fourth of the King of Prussia."*

"N. B. These are not to exceed fifteen inches in height, nor ten in width."

"2 other Busts, of Prince Eugene and the Duke of Marlborough, somewhat smaller."

"2 Wild Beasts, not to exceed twelve inches in height, nor eighteen in length."

"Sundry small ornaments for chimney-piece."

We also find Col. Washington seeking, by importations from France and England, to adorn his plantation with the graceful drapery of the

* How little did the writer imagine, when penning this order, that not many years later, his walls would be adorned by a portrait of the Great Frederick, sent him by that Monarch, and accompanied by the memorable words, "From the oldest General in Europe, to the greatest General in the world!"

blue hills of the "sunny South," and with the far-famed verdure of rural Albion.

Our readers must bear in mind that, at the period to which our narrative refers, the various domestic arrangements, of which we have, very briefly, endeavored to convey an idea, were comparatively unusual in the American Colonies; and that not only all articles of luxury, but a very great proportion of the essentials of household convenience and daily comfort, were imported from Europe. It will thus be perceived, that what would now scarcely be regarded in the light of luxurious indulgences were then within the reach only of the most wealthy. Even the clothing of his servants, and the ordinary implements of agriculture, as well as most articles of *food,* not the produce of his own plantation, were twice every year ordered by Colonel Washington from his English agents.*

* We append a somewhat amusing List of articles imported from England about this time by Col. W., which was gleaned from the voluminous "MEMORANDA" published by the indisputable authority to which we have before referred. By its perusal the reader may, perhaps, gain some incidental information respecting the dress and domestic habits of Mrs. Washington, at this period of her history, together with various indications

We may believe that the efficient and cheerful aid of MRS. WASHINGTON was not wanting in the regulation and adornment of the new home to which she found herself transferred.

We perceive, from the details of his "Life," that Col. Washington almost immediately assumed the pecuniary responsibilities devolving upon him in consequence of his marriage, together with the guardianship of Mrs. Washington's two children—a duty which he continued most faithfully and affectionately to discharge until they no longer required his care.

We find in his Letters to his agents abroad, frequent references to the business affairs of Mrs. Washington, and of John and Martha Custis, each characterized by his usual precision, regularity, and conscientiousness.

The following passages from one of these Letters will serve as illustrations of the efficient supervision exercised by this judicious friend, over the interests of the new members of his family:—

of the degree of luxury and refinement characteristic of the system of life then prevalent among the more wealthy of the Virginia Planters. See NOTE A, of the Appendix.

"To Robert Cary and Company, Merchants London.

"Mount Vernon, 20 September, 1759.

"Gentlemen,

"This will make the fourth letter I have written to you since my marriage with Mrs. Martha Custis. The two first served to cover invoices of such goods as I wanted, and to advise you at the same time of the change in her affairs, and how necessary it would be to address, for the future, all your letters, which relate to the estate of the deceased Colonel Custis, to me.

* * * * * * *

"I remark the pains you take to show the impropriety of paying the duty of the estate's tobacco. When money is wanting, it cannot be expected; but, when a sum lies in your hands, it should certainly be applied that way, as far as it will go. I likewise observe the difficulties you have met with in settling for the interest of the bank stock; but I hope that is now over, unless any part or the whole should require transferring, (when a division of the estate is made,) and then timely notice will be given; but, until this happens, it may be received and placed to the estate's credit in the usual manner.

"From this time it will be requisite, that you should raise three accounts; one for me, another for the estate, and a third for Miss Patty Custis; or, if you think it more eligible, (and I believe it will be,) make me debtor on my own account for John Parke Custis, and for Miss Martha Parke Custis, as each will have their part of the estate assigned them this fall, and the whole will remain under my management, whose particular care it shall be to distinguish always, either by letter or invoice, for whom tobaccos are shipped, and for whose use goods are imported, in order to prevent mistakes arising. The estate's credit now in your hands, may be applied towards answering the whole drafts, that have been and shall be made this year; and it must appear very plain from my former letters, as well as from what is here said, how necessary it is to send regular accounts current, that, by comparing them with the books here, satisfactory settlements may, from time to time, be made to our General Court."

But though thus relieved from the irksome and uncongenial employments incident to her previous mode of life, Mrs. Washington, doubtless, found sufficient occupation in the agreeable avocations involving the health, happiness, and education of her children; and in a general superintendence of the affairs of her household, together with the many social obligations appertaining to her position.

The present situation of Mrs. Washington closely resembled that to which she was accustomed during her former marriage. She was now, as she had previously been, the wife of a prosperous, enterprising Virginia Planter. For though still

"Bearing his blushing honors thick upon him,"

Col. Washington, for many successsive years, took no other part in public affairs than occasionally to act as a local magistrate, or as a Representative in the Provincial Legislature, of which he was a member for fifteen successive years, punctually attending each sitting, though there were, occasionally, three yearly.

Col. Washington first assumed his seat in the Virginia House of Burgesses a short time subsequent to his marriage; and, if there was needed any public confirmation of the truth, that Mrs. Washington had united her fate with that of one of the bravest and most eminent of the sons of

Virginia, it was afforded by the pleasing incidents recorded in the following paragraph:—

"By a vote of the House, the Speaker, Mr. Robinson, was directed to return their thanks to Colonel Washington, on behalf of the colony, for the distinguished military services which he had rendered to his country. As soon as Colonel Washington took his seat, Mr. Robinson, in obedience to this order, and following the impulse of his own generous and grateful heart, discharged the duty with great dignity, but with such warmth of coloring and strength of expression, as entirely confounded the young hero. He rose to express his acknowledgments for the honor; but such was his trepidation and confusion, that he could not give distinct utterance to a single syllable. He blushed, stammered, and trembled for a second; when the Speaker relieved him by a stroke of address, that would have done honor to Louis the Fourteenth in his proudest and happiest moment. 'Sit down, Mr. Washington,' said he, with a conciliating smile; 'your modesty equals your valor; and that surpasses the power of any language that I possess.'"*

* Wirt's LIFE OF PATRICK HENRY.

After the commencement of her residence at Mount Vernon, Mrs. Washington occasionally accompanied her husband in his various journeys and in his official visits at Williamsburg,—the scene of her early entrance into society, and of many of the pleasing associations of later years; but most of her time was passed at home in the care and education of her children, and in the midst of other congenial pleasures, occupations, and duties.

Everywhere honored and beloved, she continued to receive the affectionate and respectful regards of a large circle of attached and admiring friends, and to extend to each the most cordial and generous hospitality. Fortunately for both, she ever united with her husband in a genial enjoyment of this agreeable and graceful courtesy—so appropriate to their social position, and so consistent with their ample resources.*

We are indebted to Mr. Sparks for a somewhat minute sketch of several of the recipients of the hospitalities of Mount Vernon, at the time to which our narrative at present refers:—

* We learn from excellent authority, that an accession of more than one hundred thousand dollars was made to the fortune of Col. Washington by his marriage with Mrs. Custis.

"Although Col. Washington's pursuits were those of a retired farmer, yet he was by no means secluded from social intercourse with persons of intelligence and refinement. During the periods of his attending the House of Burgesses at Williamsburg, he met on terms of intimacy the eminent men of Virginia, who, in imitation of the Governors, (sometimes noblemen, and always from the higher ranks of English society,) lived in a style of magnificence, which has long passed away, and given place to the republican simplicity of modern times. He was a frequent visitor at Annapolis, the seat of government of Maryland, renowned as the resort of the polite, wealthy, and fashionable. At Mount Vernon he returned the civilities he had received, and practised, on a large and generous scale, the hospitality for which the Southern planters have ever been distinguished. When he was at home, a day seldom passed without the company of friends or strangers at the house. In his diaries the names of these visitors are often mentioned, and we find among them the Governors of Virginia and Maryland, and nearly all the celebrated men of the southern and middle colonies, who were afterwards conspicuous in the history of the country."

"One of his nearest neighbors was George Mason, of Gunston Hall, a man possessing remarkable intellectual powers, deeply conversant with political science, and thoroughly versed in the topics of dispute then existing between England and America. Lord Fairfax was also a constant guest at Mount Vernon, who, although eccentric in his habits, possessed a cultivated mind, social qualities, and a perfect knowledge of the world. To these may be added a large circle of relatives and acquaintances, who sought his society, and to whom his house was always open."

While alluding to the different sources of happiness enjoyed during this period of her life, by the estimable Subject of our Memoir, we should not omit particularly to mention the pure and exalted gratification springing from her enlightened and systematic charity, from her conscientious attention to the numerous dependants immediately relying upon her care for health and comfort, and from her habitual and devout attention to the duties of religion.*

* Both Col. and Mrs. Washington were at this time communicants in the church of the parish of Truro, in which the family estate was included, and upon the public services of which they were constant attendants. Col. W. was, also, long

Occupied by pleasures, employments, and duties of which we have thus endeavored to give our readers a passing idea, long did this excellent lady glide serenely and happily down the stream of time.

As Miss Custis, the only daughter of Mrs. Washington, advanced towards womanhood, the tender maternal assiduity that so earnestly sought her improvement in all that could tend to promote her happiness and usefulness in after life, was, if possible, still more devoted in its manifestations.

And when, at last, the child of so many hopes, the favored recipient of such accumulated care and tenderness, became the intelligent companion of the mother to whose guidance she owed so much, words are inadequate to express that mother's pride and joy.

But Mrs. Washington was destined again to behold the cup of happiness pass, scarce tasted, from her lips.

Miss Custis had no sooner attained maturity than she was snatched forever from the presence of her earthly friends.

a vestryman of this church, and a most active and useful assistant in the management of its secular affairs.

Who shall tell the sorrow of the bereaved and grief-stricken mother; the passionate lamentation of the young brother who, hand in hand with this one gentle sister, had grown in health and beauty through so many happy years of genial and loving companionship; or the deep sadness of the almost paternal guardian beneath whose fostering care her youthful mind had so pleasingly developed?

The melancholy event that thus, suddenly, robbed Mount Vernon of one of its brightest and most cherished ornaments, occurred in the year 1770.

Subsequent to this sad incident, for several successive years, nothing demanding particular notice arose to vary the usual routine of Mrs. Washington's existence.

The tender sympathy that calms and soothes the wounded heart, beyond all else that earth can give, united with the dictates of religion to soften regrets which they could not remove, and

> "Time, that wears out the trace of deepest sorrow,"

witnessed a gradual diminution of the pervading and poignant grief that long shadowed the spirit of this mourning mother.

At length, the distant murmurs of the approaching storm that served to render more dear the sanctity and the delights of home, reached ears all unwilling to receive the dreadful tidings they conveyed. Near, and yet more near, advanced the threatening clouds, till even the most incredulous were compelled to fear its fast-coming fury.

Mrs. Washington was first fully awakened to a foreboding sense of the changes that awaited her, when her husband, obeying the summons of patriotism, hastened to join in the momentous public deliberations, upon the results of which hung consequences of so much present and prospective importance. Then, indeed, she became only too surely convinced that the master-spirit had departed from the home-paradise, within which, for seventeen successive years, there had so seldom entered the sin and suffering that make the alloy of all human happiness!

CHAPTER IV.

Hark! forth from the abyss, a voice proceeds,
A long, low, distant murmur of dread sound,
Such as arises when a Nation bleeds
With some deep and immedicable wound. BYRON.

Should Heaven, yet unappeased, refuse its aid,
Disperse our hopes, and frustrate our designs,
Yet shall the conscience of the great attempt
Diffuse a brightness on our future days;
Nor will his country's groans reproach Demetrius.
JOHNSON.

WHEN Col. Washington left Mount Vernon to attend the meeting of the first Congress at Philadelphia, Mrs. Washington remained at home, participating, though at a distance, the interest and anxiety with which he discharged the various and peculiarly responsible duties which the SOLDIER OF AMERICA was directly summoned to assume; and watching with engrossing eagerness, for his reports of the highly interesting proceedings and deliberations of the solemn assemblage with which he was associated.

When, after more than nine months of separation and solitude, she was informed of her husband's appointment as Commander-in-Chief of the American Army, and that "the war had actually begun" which must summon him to immediate action, the mingled nature of her emotions may be easily conceived.

The first intelligence of this event was communicated to Mrs. Washington in the following Letter, which possesses the more interest as it is the only one of the many addressed to her from the same source, that has descended to us.*

"Philadelphia, 18 June, 1775.

"MY DEAREST:

"I am now set down to write to you on a subject, which fills me with inexpressible concern, and this concern is greatly aggravated and increased, when I reflect upon the uneasiness I know it will give you. It has been determined in Congress, that the whole army raised for the defence of the American cause shall be put under my care, and that it is necessary for me to proceed immediately to Boston to take upon me the command of it.

* It is known that Mrs. Washington, previous to her death, destroyed these precious testimonials of affection and confidence—unwilling, it may be supposed, to allow other eyes than her own to trace the cherished records.

"You may believe me, my dear Patsy, when I assure you, in the most solemn manner, that, so far from seeking this appointment, I have used every endeavor in my power to avoid it, not only from my unwillingness to part with you and the family, but from a consciousness of its being a trust too great for my capacity, and that I should enjoy more real happiness in one month with you at home, than I have the most distant prospect of finding abroad, if my stay were to be seven times seven years. But as it has been a kind of destiny, that has thrown me upon this service, I shall hope that my undertaking it is designed to answer some good purpose. You might, and I suppose did perceive, from the tenor of my letters, that I was apprehensive I could not avoid this appointment, as I did not pretend to intimate when I should return. That was the case. It was utterly out of my power to refuse this appointment, without exposing my character to such censures, as would have reflected dishonor upon myself, and given pain to my friends. This, I am sure, could not, and ought not to be pleasing to you, and must have lessened me considerably in my own esteem. I shall rely, therefore, confidently on that Providence, which has heretofore preserved and been bountiful to me, not doubting but that I shall return safe to you in the fall. I shall feel no pain from the toil or the danger of the campaign; my unhappiness will flow from the uneasiness I know you will feel from being left alone. I therefore beg that you will summon your whole fortitude, and pass your time as agreeably as possible. Nothing will give me so much sincere satisfaction as to hear this, and to hear it from your own pen. My earnest and ardent desire is, that you would pursue any plan that is most likely to produce content, and a tolerable degree of tranquillity; as it must add greatly to my uneasy feelings to hear that you are dissatisfied or complaining at what I really could not avoid.

"As life is always uncertain, and common prudence dictates to every man the necessity of settling his temporal concerns, while it is in his power, and while the mind is calm and undisturbed, I have, since I came to this place, (for I had no time to do it before I left home,) got Colonel Pendleton to draft a will for me, by the directions I gave him, which will I now enclose. The provision made for you in case of my death, will, I hope, be agreeable.

"I shall add nothing more, as I have several letters to write, but to desire that you will remember me to your friends, and to assure you that I am, with the most unfeigned regard, my dear Patsy,

"Your affectionate

"GEORGE WASHINGTON."*

The contents of this letter, will, far more effectually than any comments of ours, convey to our readers a just conception of the considerate and affectionate respect always paid by the illustrious PATER PATRIÆ to the wishes, feelings, and comfort of the celebrated Subject of our Memoir.

Though there is no allusion in this epistle to the possibility of Mrs. Washington's accompanying the Commander-in-Chief in his journey to Cambridge, nor to the prospect of even a brief reunion after this, their first protracted separation, yet it was subsequently determined that they should, temporarily at least, be relieved from the mutual pain of absence, as will be explained by the following passage from a letter addressed by Washington to his brother.

* Sparks' WRITINGS OF WASHINGTON.

"Camp at Cambridge, 13 October, 1775.

"DEAR BROTHER:

* * * * * * * * *

"I am obliged to you for your advice to my wife, and for your intention of visiting her. Seeing no great prospect of returning to my family and friends this winter, I have sent an invitation to Mrs. Washington to come to me, although I fear the season is too far advanced to admit this with any tolerable degree of convenience, especially if she should, when my letters get home, be in New Kent, as I believe the case will be. I have laid before her a statement of the difficulties, however, which must attend the journey, and left it to her own choice."*

There is no reference in this Letter to any apprehension, on the part of her husband, of danger to Mrs. Washington, should she remain at Mount Vernon, but fears for her safety were entertained by many of her friends, as we learn from the subjoined extract from Sparks' "WRITINGS OF WASHINGTON:"—

"As the General could not leave the army, he had requested Mrs. Washington to pass the win-

* Sparks' WRITINGS OF WASHINGTON.

ter with him at Cambridge. It seems, that some persons thought her in danger at Mount Vernon, which stands on the bank of the Potomac River, and is accessible to armed ships of the largest size. Lund Washington had written to the General:—'Many people have made a stir about Mrs. Washington's continuing at Mount Vernon, but I cannot think there is any danger. The thought, I believe, originated in Alexandria; from thence it got to Londoun, and I am told the people of Londoun talk of sending a guard to conduct her up to Berkeley, with some of their principal men to persuade her to leave this place, and accept their offer. Mr. John Augustine Washington wrote, pressing her to leave Mount Vernon. She does not believe herself in danger. Lord Dunmore will hardly himself venture up this river; nor do I believe he will send on that errand. Surely, her old acquaintance, the attorney, who, with his family, is on board his ship, would prevent his doing an act of that kind. You may depend I will be watchful, and upon the least alarm persuade her to remove.' "

In accordance with the wishes of her husband, Mrs. Washington hastened to make preparations for joining him at Cambridge for the winter.

Upon her arrival at Philadelphia, on her way to the scene of her new duties, she was met and escorted into the city by Col. Hancock and other officers, and the "Light Infantry of the Second Battalion, and the company of Light Horse, &c."

In addition to these public demonstrations of respect, Mrs. Washington was welcomed by every proof of individual regard and personal affection on the part of her numerous friends. She immediately received an invitation to attend a public Ball which was in contemplation, and which it was hoped the Ladies of the Commander-in Chief and of Col. Hancock would honor with their presence.

Mrs. Washington was fated thus early in her new career, to realize that Persecution, like his twin-compeer, "loves a shining mark," and that, during the commotion of public feeling which was already beginning to surge and swell, she must prepare to meet the popular tumult, manifestations of which would, thenceforth, occasionally reach even to her.

Before the evening appointed for the intended fête arrived, fears were entertained that the anticipated festivities would be disagreeably interrupted, and that the tranquillity of the city might be seriously disturbed by an occurrence, under ordinary circumstances so unimportant to the populace.

Accordingly, there was a numerous meeting of the most respectable citizens, at Philosophic Hall, "for the purpose of considering the propriety of allowing the ball to be given."—After much serious deliberation, it was finally concluded that no such entertainment should take place, either then, or "in future, while these troublesome times continued."

This meeting resulted in the appointment of a committee, whose duty it should be to desire the managers of the intended Ball to relinquish their design, and, also, to wait upon Mrs. Washington with the request that she should decline any participation in the affair.

It was understood that Mrs. Washington readily assented to the wishes of the gentlemen who called on her on this occasion, assured them of the entire accordance of her feelings with their own, in relation to the matter, and politely expressed her acknowledgments for the kind attention that had secured her against embarrassment and annoyance.*

* For the quaint version of this singular illustration of popu-

After enjoying the society of her friends for a few days, and, at the same time, refreshing herself with needful rest from the fatigue of her already long and laborious journey, Mrs. Washington left Philadelphia,* on her way to New England, "attended by the Troop of Horse, two companies of Light Infantry, &c., &c."

The anxious and affectionate care with which, despite his engrossing public duties, the Commander-in-Chief endeavored to secure the safety and comfort of Mrs. Washington, during her journey to the American Camp, is proved by the frequent references to the subject contained in his letters. Thus, in a letter to his Military Secretary, Joseph Reed, Esq., we find the following passage, under date of the 20th of November:—

"I thank you for your frequent allusions to Mrs. Washington. I expect that she will be in Philadelphia about the time this letter may reach you, on her way hither. As she and her conductor, who I suppose will be Mr. Custis, her son, are perfect strangers to the road, the stages, and the proper place to cross Hudson's River, by

lar feeling given in "Christopher Marshall's Diary of 1775," see Note B., of the Appendix.

* 27th November, 1775.

all means avoiding New York, I shall be much obliged by your particular instructions and advice to her. I imagine, as the roads are bad, and the weather cold, her stages must be short, especially as I presume her horses will be fatigued; as when they get to Philadelphia, they will have performed a journey of at least four hundred and fifty miles, my express having found her among her friends, ner Williamsburg, one hundred and fifty miles below our house."

Mrs. Washington reached Cambridge in safety on the 11th December, having accomplished the journey from Philadelphia in about fifteen days. She was soon comfortably established in the elegant mansion of one of the wealthy Tory families, who deserted their residences upon the approach of the Continental Army. The American officers, generally, took possession of these luxurious abodes, thus—and then only during the continuance of the War,—"faring sumptuously every day."

After Mrs. Washington's arrival in the American Camp, the punctilious courtesy of the Commander-in-Chief dictated the following expression of his sense of grateful obligation to the many friends whose kind attentions she had elicited during her journey.

"To Joseph Reed, Esq.

"Camp, December 25th, 1775.

"Dear Sir:

* * * * * *

"I am so much indebted for the civilities shown Mrs. Washington on her journey hither, that I hardly know how to go about to acknowledge them. Some of the enclosed (all of which I beg the favor of you to put into the post-office,) are directed to that end. I shall be obliged to you for presenting my thanks to the commanding officers of the two battalions of Philadelphia, for the honors done her and me, as also to any others equally entitled. I very sincerely offer you the compliments of the season, and wish you, Mrs. Reed, and your fireside, the happy return of a great many of them, being, dear Sir,

"Your most obedient and

"Affectionate humble servant,

"George Washington."*

It would of course, be irrelevant to our subject, as well as a work of supererogation, to attempt

* Life and Correspondence of President Reed.

a detailed account of the memorable siege and eventual evacuation of Boston.

Mrs. Washington, while participating in the harassing embarrassments that, almost directly upon the assumption of his new position, began to demand the sympathy she always exhibited in whatever affected either the interest or happiness of her husband, was now called upon to illustrate in relation to him, as she had ever done in every personal trial and affliction, her firm reliance upon the beneficent superintendence of overruling Wisdom and Goodness. Even in this early stage of his eventful military career, her habitual cheerfulness and practical abilities, served in many instances, essentially to aid and encourage the Commander-in-Chief.

The agreeable and estimable qualities of the wife of the American Hero soon won for her the love and veneration of her husband's companions in arms, and her universal popularity among them, occasioned her receiving the appellation of "*Lady Washington,*" the well-known title by which she was always afterwards distinguished in the American Army.

With the departure of the British Fleet from

the Harbor of Boston,* Mrs. Washington prepared to return to her long-deserted home,—the portentous aspect of military affairs warning her of the impracticability of remaining with the Commander-in-Chief during the season of actual hostilities.

In addition to her parting from her husband, this affectionate mother was, also, necessitated to nerve herself for a separation from her son, who was already pledged to share the military fortunes of his beloved step-father.—For usefulness and honor she had reared him to manhood, and to her country she now resigned this last lingering scion of maternal hope and joy.†

* 17th March, 1776.

† Whether or not Mr. Custis was already one of the *military family*, strictly speaking, of the Commander-in-Chief, we have not the means of determining; but we know him, together with Mrs. Custis, to have accompanied his mother to Cambridge, to have been at the siege of Boston, and to have continued with Washington throughout the war, though he probably did not, in consequence of his youth, thus early receive the appointment of *Aid-de-Camp* to the General-in-Chief.

CHAPTER V.

Employ'd she employs;
* * * * * *
* * * * * *
Locks the chest and the wardrobe, with lavender smelling,
And the hum of the spindle goes quick through the dwelling;
And she hoards in the presses, well polished and full,
The snow of the linen, the shine of the wool;
Blends the sweet with the good, and from care and endeavor
Rests never! SCHILLER.

While duty measures the regard it owes
With scrupulous precision and nice justice,
Love never reasons, but profusely gives—
Gives, like a thoughtless prodigal, its all,
And trembles then, lest it has done too little. MORE.

MRS. WASHINGTON sought the security and seclusion of Mount Vernon, not to indulge in vain repinings at her separation from its master and from her only child, nor to yield herself up to the unworthy dominion of useless fears for their personal safety and well-being; but to find in active and needful occupation, and in care for the happiness of others, the best guarantee afforded by circumstances, for the preservation of her mental serenity.

That knowledge of practical life, and that singular facility for adapting herself to avocations unusual to her sex, which she had exhibited during her widowhood, were now again called into exercise by the peculiar situation in which Mrs. Washington found herself placed. She immediately established a domestic system thoroughly adapted to the exigencies of the times, and eminently calculated as an example most beneficially to influence others. Her dress,—always remarkable for its simplicity,—was soon composed almost entirely of home-made materials, as was the clothing of her numerous domestics.

We have her own authority for the fact that "she had a great deal of domestic cloth made in her house," and that "sixteen spinning-wheels were kept in constant operation" at Mount Vernon. One one occasion, when conversing with some friends upon this and similar topics, she gave the best proof of her success in domestic manufactures by the exhibition of two of her dresses, which were composed of cotton striped with silk, and entirely home-made. The silk stripes in the fabric were woven from "the ravellings of brown silk stockings and old crimson damask chair-covers!"

Momentarily to anticipate in our narrative;—when Washington arrived at New York to assume his duties as first President of the United States, he was attired in a complete suit of home-spun cloth.

By the judicious and admirable simplicity and economy she systematically practiced, this exemplary Revolutionary matron secured the means, not only of personal and domestic comfort, convenience, and independence, but of the benevolent diffusion of more generally extended benefit.

It must not be supposed, however, that these household avocations and duties were sufficient to engross, or content, one whose interest in the progress of public events was so painfully augmented by her intimate connection with the master-spirit upon whose wisdom and guidance hung the destiny of his country.

Mrs. Washington was, doubtless, kept well and promptly advised not only of the momentous events that followed each other in such rapid and startling succession, during the ever-memorable year succeeding the siege of Boston, but of the individual adventures and personal feelings and apprehensions of her husband. The asseverations and fears expressed in the following sentences were, probably, often repeated in Washington's frequent letters to this sympathizing recipient of his confidence:—"I am wearied to death with the retrograde motion of things, and I solemnly protest that a pecuniary reward of twenty thousand pounds would not induce me to undergo what I do."* "In a word, if every nerve is not strained to recruit the new army with all possible expedition, *the game is nearly up.*"†

Only a wife as devoted as Mrs. Washington, can fully appreciate her emotions of indignation and abhorrence, when made acquainted with the happily-discovered treachery that aimed at the personal safety of the Commander-in-Chief, and the success of which would have dealt a death-blow to the prosperity of the American Cause. Only such a one can realize the pride and pleasure that swelled in her heart, when informed of the glorious passage of the Delaware, and of the encouraging success of which that skilful manœ-

* Washington to his Brother, 19th Nov. 1776—Sparks' WRITINGS OF WASHINGTON.

† Washington to his Brother, 18th Dec. 1776—LIFE AND CORRESPONDENCE OF PRESIDENT REED.

uvre was the immediate precursor; or paint the harrowing anxiety with which she awaited further intelligence respecting the movements of the little Continental Army; and her delight when certain of the temporary cessation of active hostilities, and of the consequent safety of those most dear to her. But why attempt to particularize among incidents, each of which was necessarily invested with such vital importance for this tender Mother, this sympathizing Wife, this patriotic American Matron!

CHAPTER VI.

To paint that being to a grovelling mind
Were like portraying pictures to the blind.
'Twas needful e'en infectiously to feel
Her temper's fond and firm and gladsome zeal,
To share existence with her, and to gain
Sparks from her love's electrifying chain,
Of that pure pride, which lessening to her breast
Life's ills, gave all its joys a treble zest,
Before the mind completely understood
That mighty truth—how happy are the good! CAMPBELL.

WHEN the American Commander-in-Chief, after ten months of incessant exertion, fatigue, and responsibility that succeeded their parting, immediately subsequent to the evacuation of Boston, had finally conducted his worn and weary Army into winter quarters, at Morristown, in New Jersey,* MRS. WASHINGTON, anxious for his health and comfort as well as for those of her son, lost no time in repairing thither to join him in the Camp for the remainder of the season.

It became, thenceforth, during the continuance of the War of the Revolution, Mrs. Washington's

* Jan. 1777.

habitual practice to pass her winters at the Head-quarters of the American Army. It was, consequently, her wont to say, in after life, that "she had heard the first cannon at the opening and the last at the closing of all the campaigns of the Revolution!"

Many passages in the private Letters of Washington express his affectionate interest on the subject of Mrs. Washington's long and hazardous journeys at the inclement season of the year when they were, necessarily, undertaken. We find him writing to ask advice as to the best means of promoting her safety and comfort, or requesting assistance in effecting her transit from Mount Vernon to him, and again, expressing his thanks for the many civilities extended to her on such occasions by friends whose personal and patriotic devotion, no considerations of policy or prudence could vary or diminish.

Mrs. Washington's journeys to the American Camp were always performed in her own carriage and attended by her own servants. It was, also, the invariable practice of the Commander-in-Chief, to dispatch one of his Aids-de-Camp to escort her from Mount Vernon to his Winter quarters.* We infer, that on some of these occasions, at least, he adopted the additional precaution to dispatch a band of soldiers, the more effectually to insure her protection, as we are told that in one instance, when travelling, Mrs. Washington's chariot was attended by ten dragoons, and that, at another time, her departure from Philadelphia was accompanied by two military companies.

The example of the wife of the American General-in-Chief, in passing the winters with her husband in his Camp quarters, was generally imitated by the wives of the principal officers of the Continental Army; and her arrival soon came to be regarded as a signal for the assemblage of the fair ministering spirits whose presence lent a charm even to hardship and danger.

The following anecdote, for which, as well as for some other details, we are indebted to the elegant and highly entertaining volumes of Mrs. Ellet, will serve to illustrate the unwearying and affectionate zeal with which Mrs. Washington was herself befriended by those towards whom

* As one of the Military Family of Washington, we may suppose that a duty, for many reasons so peculiarly agreeable to him, was, at least occasionally, delegated to Col. Custis.

she was so ready to exhibit the most substantial proofs of her regard and interest:—

"There were but two frame houses in the settlement (where Washington had established his Winter quarters) and neither had a finished upper story. The General was contented with his rough dwelling, but wished to prepare for his wife a more retired and comfortable apartment. He sent for the young mechanic, who was himself many years afterwards the narrator of the incident, and desired him and one of his fellow-apprentices to fit up a room in the upper story for the accommodation of Lady Washington through the winter. She herself arrived before the work was commenced. "She came," says the military carpenter, "into the place—a portly-looking, agreeable woman of forty-five, and said to us: 'Now, young men, I care for nothing but comfort here; and should like you to fit me up a beaufet on one side of the room, and some shelves and places for hanging clothes on the other.' We went to work with all our might. Every morning about eleven, Mrs. Washington came up stairs with a glass of spirits for each of us; and after she and the General had dined, we were called down to eat at their table. We worked very hard, nailing smooth boards over the rough and worm-eaten planks, and stopping the crevices in the walls made by time and hard usage. We then consulted together how we could smooth the uneven floor, and take out, or cover over some of the huge black knots. We studied to do everything to please so pleasant a lady, and to make some return in our humble way, for the kindness of the General. On the fourth day, when Mrs. Washington came up to see how we were getting along, we had finished the work, made the shelves, put up the pegs in the wall, built the beaufet, and converted the rough garret into a comfortable apartment. As she stood looking round, I said, 'Madam, we have endeavored to do the best we could; I hope we have suited you.' She replied, smiling, 'I am astonished! your work would do honor to an old master, and you are mere lads. I am not only satisfied, but highly gratified by what you have done for my comfort.'"

Those who had the happiness to be able to speak and write from personal knowledge, bore the most unequivocal and emphatic testimony to the benign influence diffused through the Camp by the welcome presence of "LADY WASHINGTON." Her cheerfulness and equanimity were happily and habitually displayed, even in the most trying circumstances, and exerted over the minds of all who were so fortunate as to share her friendship, or participate in her benevolent cares, the most beneficial effect.

> "———And to know her well
> Prolong'd, exalted, bound, enchantment's spell;
> For with affections warm, intense, refined,
> She mix'd such calm and holy strength of mind,
> That, like heaven's image in the smiling brook,
> Celestial peace was pictured in her look.
> Her's was the brow, in trials unperplex'd,
> That cheer'd the sad, and tranquillized the vex'd;
> She studied not the meanest to eclipse,
> And yet the wisest listened to her lips."—

She submitted with the utmost patience to personal privation and hardship, and did the honors of her homely camp abode with all the grace and urbanity that had formerly distinguished the mistress of the White House and of Mount Vernon. Her unwavering religious faith and her perpetual serenity and good humor, not only contributed materially to the general good, but were of great service to her husband individually. The Commander-in-Chief, both by word and action, gave ample proof that the habits of military life were far from diminishing his affection for the companion of more genial hours, or his just appreciation of the advantages arising to himself from her society. As an illustration in point, some of our readers will recollect, that, when on one occasion, while this courageous woman and her fair companions still remained in their martial homes, and there was a sudden apprehension that "the enemy" were rapidly approaching, Washington resisted the proposition made by his military friends, to send the ladies away under an escort;—saying, "The presence of our wives will better encourage us to a brave defence!"

"Lady Washington's" time and attention during each of the many seasons of her residence with the Army—apart from the dearer duties and obligations arising out of her reunions with her husband and son—were chiefly devoted to the humane purposes of benefiting and relieving the suffering soldiers. She visited the sick, ministered to their wants, and poured that sympathy which is the "oil of joy" into their desponding hearts. She is described by those who witnessed and partook her efforts, as having been unwavering in her zeal and earnestness in this, her noble and womanly purpose. No danger delayed, no difficulty or hardship prevented the fulfilment of these benevolent duties. Blessings and prayers followed the departure of this beneficent spirit from among the recipients of her kindness and bounty, and the most heartfelt delight hailed her return!

Nor were the winters thus passed by this estimable wife and mother wholly wanting in other sources of merely personal enjoyment, than those arising from her constant association with the objects of her deepest affections. She became closely and confidentially connected with the noble and heroic women, who, like herself, were pledged to the service of their country—those *private defenders* of the Cause of Liberty, whose dearest interests, whose highest hopes, whose all, in short, of earthly happiness was involved in the issue of passing events.

The friendships thus fostered by propinquity, and cemented by strong congeniality of sentiment and interest, as well as by the bond of common danger and suffering, in addition to the present sympathy and enjoyment to which they gave rise, were among the most cherished pleasures of Mrs. Washington's subsequent life.

When separated from these valued friends by

the vicissitudes of the active campaigns, in which during each season the nearest relatives of all were equally engaged and endangered, it was the solace and gratification of each, by a constant correspondence, not only to maintain their mutual remembrance and affection, but to uphold and encourage each other in the Good Cause, by a more zealous *esprit du corps* than ever cemented the secret compact of

"——a band of brothers joined!"*

It is to be much regretted that only detached fragments of Mrs. Washington's correspondence have been preserved to the present day. The following extract from an epistle addressed by her

* Our fair readers must not suppose that "Lady Washington," or any other lady of her day, enjoyed during the Revolution, the advantages of a regular, safe, systematic Post-Office arrangement. This was far enough from being the case. Not unfrequently the Commander-in-Chief, in addition to his other multitudinous avocations, acted as Post-Master General for his female friends and their lords or lovers.—But, in spite of chance accidents, difficulties, and delays, the active minds that were roused to such high tension by the powerful stimulus of the times, found passing relief and amusement in this agreeable mode of interchanging sentiment, feelings, and more particular intelligence in relation to matters and occurrences generally and individually interesting.

to a female friend, will serve to indicate the spirit by which she was habitually actuated in similar circumstances:—

"It gives me unspeakable pleasure to hear that General Burgoyne and his army are in safe quarters in your State. Would bountiful Providence aim a like blow at General Howe, the measure of my happiness would be complete!"

In addition to much pleasing intercourse with her own sex, it was the good fortune of this patriot wife to enjoy the friendship and society of her husband's most distinguished military companions. It was her high privilege to share in their councils, and imbibe their exalted sentiments, to participate in their self-denial, their zeal, their enthusiasm, and their courage! There were Steuben, Rochambeau, La Fayette, Kosciusko, and a host of heroes "to the manor born,"—Knox, and Greene, and Putnam, and Moultrie, and Hamilton, and many others, of less note, perchance, but lofty and glorious spirits all, amidst whom, as one enshrined by yet higher purpose and yet more august intellect,

> "in shape and gesture proudly eminent,
> Stood like a tower"

the beloved and illustrious PATER PATRIÆ with

whom it was her pride and happiness to be united by ties so tender, so endearing, and so blessed!

Thus, then, though surrounded by discomfort, subjected to trials, sorrows, and sufferings, called to witness and to partake apprehensions, cares, and responsibilities, in their results at once the most engrossing and the most important, it was to those portions of her existence which were passed in the Camp of the heroic Army of the Revolution, that Mrs. Washington could, in after years, revert, as having afforded some of the happiest hours of her life!—hours of enjoyment so pure, so exalted, so spiritual, that there was

"——less of earth in them than Heaven!"

CHAPTER VII.

The field of freedom, faction, fame, and blood:
Here a proud people's passions were exhaled,
From the first hour of empire in the bud. BYRON.

——If the consciousness of perpetual endeavor to advance our race be not alone happier than the life of ease, let us see what this vaunted ease really is. Tell me, is it not another name for *ennui?* This state of quiescence, this objectless, dreamless torpor, this transition *du lit a la table, de la table au lit;* what more dreary and monotonous existence can you devise? Is it pleasure in this inglorious existence to think that you are serving pleasure? Is it freedom to be the slave of self?

PILGRIMS OF THE RHINE.

WE resume our somewhat interrupted narrative of the events of MRS. WASHINGTON'S life, with that of her return to Mount Vernon, in the Spring of 1777, after her first thorough initiation into the hardships, privations, and sufferings of the American Camp, during the winter passed by her in the log hut that constituted her abode at Morristown.

This interval of leisure for home duties and avocations, was, much of it, passed, like that of the previous season, in arrangements for the well-being of the relatives and domestics dependent upon her care and guidance.

We gather from the private Correspondence of Washington, that he maintained, throughout his protracted absence from home, the general supervision and direction of affairs relative to his plantation; but it will readily be supposed that the skill and judgment displayed by this eminently-practical woman, when she was but little more than twenty years of age, in the exclusive management of a large landed estate, were now of most essential service in promoting the proper management of all out-of-door matters, as well as of those of a merely household character. The gloomy aspect of public affairs rendered the prospect of her husband's ability to resume the personal care of his private affairs more and more remote and uncertain, and Mrs. Washington was, consequently, impressed with the necessity of so regulating her family arrangements as to supply, in a degree, at least, the place of their absent master to those employed in his service, or dependent upon his bounty.

When winter approached, this heroic and devoted wife was prepared again to return to the companionship of her husband, and to re-assume the interesting and benevolent offices she had appropriated to herself.

This was, as our readers will remember, the terrible winter of 1777–78, which witnessed the frightful sufferings of our Army at Valley Forge, where, "while the foe were luxuriating in the comfortable quarters of a populous and luxurious city, the Americans were sheltered in huts of their own fabrication, and frequently suffering the extremity of want."*

The following brief passage from one of Mrs. Washington's letters, written at this time, contains a passing description of her camp accommodations :—"The General's apartment is very small; he has had a log cabin built to dine in, which has made our quarters more tolerable than they were at first."

Thus, then, did this high-souled and self-sacrificing woman voluntarily exchange the ease, the comfort, and the security of her home, for incon-

* Valley Forge is six miles above Norristown, in Pennsylvania, on the west side of the Schuylkill river, and about twenty miles from Philadelphia. It is a deep, rugged hollow, at the mouth of Valley Creek, from which, and from an ancient *forge* once established there, it takes its name. On the mountain sides of this wild spot, Washington fixed the camp of the American Army during the winter of 1777–78.

venience, privation, and danger, that she might the better sympathize with, and minister to her husband; who, oppressed by conflicting duties, difficulties, and trials, and, at the same time, a mark for the shafts of public animadversion and private intrigue, could turn trustingly to the faithful and tender friend who was ever ready to share his cares, his anxieties, and his toils.

True to the faith and fortitude of a Christian, side by side with her heroic husband, did she stem alike the tide of popular discontent and the tumultuous commotion more immediately surrounding her in the Camp. Unappalled by the disaffection, persecution, mortality, and despair by which she was environed, she was content to endure all, brave all, save separation from the cherished objects of her warmest affections.

Calm, cheerful, hopeful, her presence and her example shed light and blessing even upon the deepest gloom and the most fearful horrors!

The last ensanguined record of this ever-memorable winter was at length traced upon the Page of Time!

Well has it been said, that, in the moral, as in the physical world, the darkest hour precedes that of dawning light. The calumnies by which the

Commander-in-Chief had been so ruthlessly assailed, only served to elicit the strongest proofs of public confidence and individual attachment. The cruel deprivations and sufferings of the Patriot Soldiers were now materially relieved. Eager preparation and active discipline took the place of discontent and despondency. And bright-eyed May, the fairy-footed daughter of the year, was a welcome harbinger of the inspiring intelligence that France had publicly recognized the Independence of the American Republic, and that her efficient aid would now assist the struggling cause of Liberty!

"A day was set apart for a public celebration in camp. It began in the morning with religious services, and a discourse to each of the brigades by one of its chaplains. Then followed military parades, marchings, and firings of cannon and musketry, according to a plan announced in the general orders. The appearance was brilliant, and the effect imposing. The whole ceremony was conducted with perfect regularity, and was closed with an entertainment, patriotic toasts, music, and other demonstrations of joy."

The following paragraph from the pen of an

enthusiastic letter-writer* graphically portrays the encouraging aspect of affairs in the Republican Camp after the reception of the soul-cheering news of our National Alliance with the Land of La Fayette:—"We have nothing here but rejoicing; every one looks happy, and seems proud of the share he has had in humbling the pride of Britain, and of establishing the name of America as a nation."

Sir Henry Clinton's evacuation of Philadelphia was the signal for the breaking up of the American Camp at Valley Forge.

Mrs. Washington once more returned to the scene of her long-interrupted domestic felicity, again to encounter the suspense, the forebodings, the alternating hopes and fears, that must, inevitably, fall to the lot of one watching at a distance from the scene of action, the changeful indications of the political horizon, and far separated from those who rendered both her home and her country doubly dear to her heart.

Our brief and imperfect description of the most prominent characteristics of the Winter

* Lady Catherine Alexander, writing from Valley Forge to a friend.

passed at Valley Forge by the illustrious Subject of our narrative, will serve, in its general features, as a type of those of many succeeding years.

The Head-Quarters of the Commander-in-Chief were for several seasons established on the banks of the Hudson, or in its vicinity, more or less near to New York, as circumstances permitted. And Mrs. Washington continued, throughout the war, to make each year a long and hazardous journey ere she could rejoin her husband and son, and, as often, voluntarily to encounter many consecutive months of fatigue, exposure, and deprivation.

The sprightly sketch* that follows, not only possesses much interest from its furnishing the outline of a day passed by the writer, the Marquis de Chastellux, as the guest of Gen. and Mrs. Washington, in their military home; but also, serves, incidentally, to illustrate the ingenious results to which hospitality and necessity unitedly brought the domestic resources of camp-life, under the practical superintendence of "Lady Washington." It is possible that the dwelling here

* We are indebted to Mrs. Ellet for this extract,—she herself quotes it from a *MS. Letter*.

described is the same referred to in a previous chapter, as having undergone some improvements and repairs, for the better accommodation of its fair and gentle mistress:—

"The Head-Quarters at Newburgh consist of a single house, built in the Dutch fashion, and neither large nor commodious. The largest room in it, which General Washington has converted into his dining-room, is tolerably spacious, but it has seven doors, and only one window. The chimney is against the wall; so that there is, in fact, but one vent for the smoke, and the fire is in the room itself. I found the company assembled in a small room, which served as a parlor. At nine, supper was served, and when bed-time came I found that the chamber to which the General conducted me, was the very parlor spoken of, wherein he had made them place a camp-bed. We assembled at breakfast the next morning at ten, during which interval my bed was folded up; and my chamber became the sitting-room for the whole afternoon; for American manners do not admit of a bed in the room in which company is received, especially where there are women. The smallness of the house, and the inconvenience to which I saw that General and Mrs. Washington had put themselves to receive me, made me apprehensive lest M. Rochambeau might arrive on the same day. The day I remained at head-quarters was passed either at table or in conversation."*

As we have before intimated, the wife of the American General-in-Chief, though individually so unoffending, was occasionally the subject of manifestations of the height to which party animosity rose in those troubled times.

In one of her annual removals from Mount Vernon, at the conclusion of the active campaign, Mrs. Washington's usual visit at Philadelphia was marked by great coldness on the part of the ladies resident there, many of whom forbode to call upon her during her stay in the city.†

But in agreeable contrast to treatment like this, was the cordial hospitality with which this

* It may be new to some of our readers that the house designated in this description is still standing entire at Newburgh. It is plainly discernible from the deck of a steamer upon the Hudson, and may be thus seen by the passing traveller. Long may this classic spot be sacred from the approach of the Destroyer!

† This indication of popular feeling probably grew out of the opposition made by the Philadelphians to Washington's going into winter quarters during the inclement winter of '77–78.

patriotic wife was very frequently greeted in the course of her yearly pilgrimages, by those devoted friends of the Revolutionary cause at whose several residences she was temporarily entertained.

We are told by a graceful annalist, that, on one occasion, when the Head-Quarters of the Republican Commander-in-Chief were for a short time established at the hospitable mansion of Mrs. Barry, in New Jersey, a Ball was given by the hostess to signalize the arrival of the wife of her illustrious guest. When the well-known chariot of "Lady Washington," with her coachman and postilion, in their neat white and scarlet liveries, arrived at her door, and Mrs. Barry saw a female alight, dressed in a simple "russet gown" with a "white handkerchief neatly folded over her neck," she was surprised to perceive the Hero-Chief advance to receive her, and to learn that this unostentatious stranger was none other than "*Lady Washington*"! The first salutations over (so runs the history) the General proceeded to make inquiries respecting the well-being of his favorite carriage-horses, and concluded the pleasures of the day, by treading—for the first time in a very long while—*a minuet at the Ball!*

This, at that time, a very frequent and favorite mode of celebrating a joyful occurrence, was also adopted on the Anniversary of the National Alliance with France.

"The entertainment was given in the Camp near Middlebrook. On this festive occasion Mrs. Washington, Mrs. Greene and Mrs. Knox, and the wives of several officers were present; and a circle of brilliants, the least of which was more valuable than the stone which the King of Portugal received from his Brazilian possessions. The ladies and gentlemen from a large circle around the camp, attended the celebration. It was opened by a discharge of cannon: and dinner was served in a building used for an academy. There was dancing in the evening, and a grand display of fire-works. The Ball was opened by General Washington. As this was a festival given by men who had not enriched themselves by the war, the illuminations were on a cheap scale, being entirely of their own manufacture; the seats were adorned with no armorial blazonry, but were the work of native and rather unskilful artisans. Instead of knights of different orders, such as pageants like the Mischianza could boast, there were but hardy soldiers; happy, however, in the consciousness that they had contributed to bring about the auspicious event they had met to celebrate."*

If sometimes subjected to unmerited neglect in her own country, indications were not wanting of the respect and regard entertained for Mrs. Washington abroad. Some ladies who came from New York to the American Camp, at one time, when it was fixed near that city, reported that a vessel which had been captured and brought into port, had on board a present from the Queen of France to Mrs. Washington, which was designed to manifest her interest in that lady, and to serve as "an elegant testimonial of her approbation of the General's conduct." The Marquis de La Fayette was requested by Washington to make inquiries, through the Marchioness, at Versailles, respecting this somewhat interesting matter, but we are unable to gratify our readers by relating the result of the investigation.

Scenes and incidents like these, occasionally relieved, for a brief space, the weight of care and solicitude that, despite her apparent cheerfulness and tranquillity, long rested upon the mind

* Remembrancer, Vol. VI.

of this magnanimous and patriotic American Matron.

Mrs. Washington's mental firmness and constancy of purpose were, more than once during the struggle of the Revolution, severely tested by the illness of her husband, who, taxed both in body and mind beyond the power of human endurance, was on several occasions constrained to resign himself wholly to her gentle and efficacious ministrations.

Occurrences and alarms similar to those which form the subject of the following letter, not unfrequently united with her apprehensions respecting the health of her husband to disturb the mental quietude of this exemplary wife:—

"Trenton, April 11th, 1781.

"DEAR SIR:

"I was told a few days ago by a man who had made his escape from New York, after having been thirteen months a prisoner with the enemy, that I might depend upon it there were four parties out to *take* or *assassinate* General Washington, your Excellency, me, and a fourth person, whose name he did not hear, or had forgot. As I frequently receive accounts of this kind of expedition against myself, which sometimes prove true and sometimes otherwise, I paid no great attention to the man's report. I yesterday received a letter from General Washington, dated the 8th instant, in which there is this paragraph:—'Intelligence has been sent me by a gentleman living near the enemy's lines, and who has an opportunity of knowing what passes among them, that four parties had been sent out with orders to *take* or *assassinate* your Excellency, Governor Clinton, me, and a fourth person, name not known.'

"It seems, therefore, highly probable that the gentleman whose name my informant did not remember, was Governor Clinton, and the gentleman whose name was not transmitted to General Washington, is your Excellency.

"This confirmation of my intelligence gives the matter so serious an aspect, that I think it my duty to advise your Excellency of what has come to my knowledge, that you may take such precautions on the occasion as appear to you necessary. I have the honor to be, with the greatest esteem, Dear Sir, your Excellency's

"Most humble, &c.,

"W. LIVINGSTON."*

* From Governor Livingston to President Reed.—LIFE AND CORRESPONDENCE OF PRESIDENT REED, Vol. 2, 337.

In addition to trials thus peculiarly severe, Mrs. Washington's own health was, not unfrequently, seriously impaired by the hardships of her mode of life in the camp. She had, during one winter, the fortitude to submit to the imperative ordeal of being *inoculated for the small-pox*,—the popular course in the then imperfect state of medical science,—rather than to secure safety in distance from the immediate scene of the ravages of that appalling malady.

The personal appearance of Mrs. Washington, at this meridian period of her life, is thus described by one of her friends:—"She is about forty, or five and forty, rather plump, but fresh, and of an agreeable countenance."

Time rolled on. The diligent industry of the mistress of Mount Vernon, the society of her daughter-in-law* and of the little prattlers who now began to claim her care and affection, to-

* The marriage of Colonel Custis occurred previous to, or about the time of the commencement of the Revolution, as we learn from Mr. Sparks, that her daughter-in-law accompanied Mrs. Washington to Cambridge in 1775. Though we may not enter the sacred precincts of private life in search of details respecting this event, none will question the interest with which it was invested for so affectionate a mother as Mrs. Washington.

gether with her extensive correspondence, and the never-ceasing duties of hospitality, combined to beguile the tedium of her annual separations from her almost idolized "chief;" and her winters continued to pass as they had invariably done since the commencement of the Revolution.

Faint streakings of the morning light destined to break into the effulgence of an all-glorious day, began at length to cheer the friends and defenders of Liberty, and the self-sacrificing Wife of the immortal Soldier of America rejoiced, with noble exultation, in the anticipated consummation of a Nation's freedom, achieved by *him!* Visions of domestic felicity once more delighted her mental gaze—visions of a blissful reunion with each member of her now scattered family, *at home,* in their beloved Mount Vernon, not one link wanting in the golden circlet of love, each face radiant with happiness, each heart overflowing with gratitude and affection!

> "Joy quickens her pulse, all her hardships seem o'er,
> And the voices of lov'd ones reply to her call!"

Alas, for the vanity of all human expectations! An impenetrable pall was fated suddenly to shroud from her eagerly-expectant eyes alike the triumphant success of her husband, and the dawning glory of her country.

What were all earthly honors and triumphs to a mother abruptly summoned to attend the last hours of her only remaining child!—the pride and joy of her tender and loving heart, stricken down,—not victor-crowned and dying for his country on the field of fame,—but the victim of insidious disease!

Colonel Custis had, from the commencement of the Revolutionary struggle, attached himself to the fortunes of his country, and participated, as one of the Aids-de-Camp of his step-father, in the dangers, efforts, and trials of that eventful contest. While engaged in his military duties during the siege of Yorktown, he was attacked by the malignant fever then raging in the British camp, and, after enjoying the high satisfaction of beholding the surrender of Lord Cornwallis, was immediately removed, under the superintending care of a kind and valued family friend, Dr. Craik, the Chief of the American Medical Staff, to Eltham, in New Kent.

Thither, when informed of his alarming condition, Mrs. Washington flew on the wings of tortured affection.

For the victorious American Chief, too, the cup of joyful thanksgiving was deeply tinctured with bitterness.—"*Providence left him childless that he might be the father of his country,*"* but he was strongly attached to this his almost-son, so long and so affectionately associated with him in the closest personal and official relations. He was no sooner aware of the increasing illness of Colonel Custis, than he "privately left the camp before Yorktown, while it yet rang with the shouts of victory, and, attended by a single officer, rode with all speed to Eltham."

Day was dawning upon the dimmed eyes of the agonized watchers by the bedside of the expiring sufferer, when Dr. Craik was requested to attend the Commander-in-Chief, who had just arrived.

Washington inquired whether there was any reason to hope for Colonel Custis' recovery. When the physician sadly intimated that all was nearly over, the sorrowing *pater patriæ,* retiring to a solitary apartment, threw himself upon a couch, overpowered by the most painful emotion.

* This exquisite atticism appeared originally in the form of *a toast* given at a public dinner, but the writer is not so fortunate as to know the name of its felicitous author.

When death had concluded the vigil of the an guish-stricken parent, her sympathizing husband sought her presence; and these tender friends long mingled their grief together, ere the General-in-Chief,—nerving himself to imperative effort and calmness,—returned to the world that claimed him, leaving the childless mother *alone with her God!*

CHAPTER VIII.

In Duty's active round each day is past,
As if she thought each day might prove her last:
Her labors for devotion best prepare,
And meek Devotion smooths the brow of care. MORE.

Where is the smile unfeign'd, the jovial welcome,
Which cheer'd the sad, beguil'd the pilgrim's pain,
And made Dependency forget its bonds?
Where is the ancient, hospitable hall,
Whose vaulted roof once rung with harmless mirth,
Where every passing stranger was a guest,
And every guest a friend? MORE.

AFTER the death of her son, which was, as we have seen, coeval with the virtual termination of the War of the Revolution,* the cares and affections of MRS. WASHINGTON were centered more continuously than they had been for many previous years at Mount Vernon, which was now the home of her widowed daughter-in-law and of her four little grand-children, who became, thenceforth, the objects of her especial attention and solicitude.

It was now the chief delight and blessing of her bereaved and affectionate heart to

* Oct., 1781.

"—— hear the gladsome sound
Of infant voices sweet,
The gush of fairy laughter,
Or the tread of tiny feet."

In addition to the dear and interesting companions who were added permanently to the members of her household, Mrs. Washington continued, as she had hitherto done, when at Mount Vernon during the warmer months of the year, to gather round her those other family friends and connections who had long partaken her hospitality. Sorrow had never the effect to render her selfish; nor did she now forget what was due in this respect to her husband, as well as to her own personal obligations and attachments. But she was, of course, altogether disinclined to participate in the public rejoicings and festivities in which the Republican Commander-in-Chief was compelled by his public station to take part.

It was not until after the formal conclusion of the Treaty of Peace, in 1783, that the multiplied domestic occupations and responsibilities so long resting upon Mrs. Washington, were again shared by her husband.

His public duties resigned at last, and the pain of the pathetic and sublime scene of his final parting with his beloved companions in arms encountered and passed, Mrs. Washington proceeded as far as Annapolis to meet the retiring Cincinnatus, and they returned together to the peaceful retreat from which so many revolving years, and so many momentous occurrences had separated its illustrious master.

It was on the eve of the great Jubilee of Christendom, that WASHINGTON, "an older man,"—to use his own expressive words,—"by nine years than when he left them," once more crossed his own threshold, and, beside his own hearth-stone, hailed the welcome joys of home! "The scene is at length closed," said the august Father of his Country, "I feel myself eased of a load of public care, and hope to spend the remainder of my days in cultivating the affections of good men, and in the practice of domestic virtues!"

We leave our readers to imagine the glad enthusiasm that expressed the general delight of relatives, friends, and dependants, at the long-looked-for arrival of this grand epoch in the family history of the inmates of Mount Vernon; and the more quiet, but not therefore less heartfelt, enjoyment and gratitude of Mrs. Washington, on that happy Christmas Day, when a double zest was lent, each to the other, by the combined pleasures of gratified affection and fervent devotion. The soul of a religious being, when thus blessed, must ever

"—— take Devotion's wing;
And, like the bird that hails the sun,
Far soar towards Heaven;"

and this sincere and devout Christian had too long and too unceasingly been accustomed to bear both her joys and griefs to the Cross of the Redeemer, not now to unite "the cup of thanksgiving" with her "sorrowful tears."

The following pleasing sketch* of the mode of life contemplated with cordial anticipations of gratification by the *Hero of America*, upon his return to Mount Vernon, will also serve as a correct portraiture of the tastes and wishes of his amiable home-companion:—

"At length, my dear Marquis, I am become a private citizen on the banks of the Potomac; and under the shadow of my own vine and fig-tree, free from the bustle of a camp, and the busy

* Extracted from a Letter written by Washington to La Fayette, Feb. 1, 1784.—Sparks' WRITINGS OF WASHINGTON, Vol. IX. 17.

scenes of public life, I am solacing myself with those tranquil enjoyments, of which the soldier, who is ever in pursuit of fame, the statesman, whose watchful days and sleepless nights are spent in devising schemes to promote the welfare of his own, perhaps the ruin of other countries, as if this globe was insufficient for us all, and the courtier, who is always watching the countenance of his prince, in hopes of catching a gracious smile, can have very little conception. I have not only retired from all public employments, but I am retiring within myself, and shall be able to view the solitary walk, and tread the paths of private life with a heartfelt satisfaction. Envious of none, I am determined to be pleased with all; and this, my dear friend, being the order of my march, I will move gently down the stream of life, until I sleep with my fathers."

Once thoroughly re-established in the beloved home of their earlier, and happy years, Genera and Mrs. Washington assiduously turned their attention to the enlargement of the family mansion, which still retained its original size, and to the further improvement and adornment of the adjoining grounds and gardens, all of which soon gave token of the taste, skill, and industry of both.*

"Having arranged and systematized his agricultural operations, Washington now set himself at work in earnest to execute his purpose of planting and adorning the grounds around the mansion-house. In the direction of the left wing, and at a considerable distance, was a vegetable garden; and on the right, at an equal distance, was another garden for ornamental shrubs, plants, and flowers. Between these gardens, in front of the house, was a spacious lawn, surrounded by serpentine walks. Beyond the gardens and lawn were the orchards. Very early in the spring, he began with the lawn, selecting the choicest trees from the woods on his estate, and transferring them to the borders of the serpentine walks, arranging them in such a manner as to produce symmetry and beauty in the general effect, intermingling in just proportions forest trees, evergreens, and flowering shrubs. He attended personally to the selection, removal, and planting of every tree; and his Diary, which is very particular from day to day through the whole process,

* At this time, the approach to this celebrated residence was through three successive miles of uninterrupted forest.

proves that he engaged in it with intense interest, and anxiously watched each tree and shoot till it showed signs of renewed growth. Such trees as were not found on his own lands, he obtained from other parts of the country, and at length his design was completed according to his wishes.

"The orchards, gardens, and green-houses were next replenished with all the varieties of rare fruit-trees, vegetables, shrubs, and flowering plants which he could procure. This was less easily accomplished; but, horticulture being with him a favorite pursuit, he continued during his life to make new accessions of fruits and plants, both native and exotic."

Apart from these agreeable employments, in which she occasionally took part, Mrs. Washington found ample occupation in the charge of a large household, which was constantly augmented by the addition of numerous guests.

The following letter furnishes pleasing proof of the thoughtful and sympathizing kindness with which her ever-considerate husband sought to relieve the mistress of Mount Vernon, at least in part, from the onerous labors of housekeeping:—

"Mount Vernon, 7th Sept., 1785.

"SIR:

"As no person can judge better of the qualifications necessary to constitute a good housekeeper, or household steward, than yourself, for a family which has a good deal of company, and wishes to entertain them in a plain, but genteel style, I take the liberty of asking you, if there is any such one within your reach, whom you think could be induced to come to me on reasonable wages. I would rather have a man than a woman, but either will do, if they can be recommended for their honesty, sobriety, and knowledge of their profession; which, in one word, is to relieve Mrs. Washington from the drudgery of ordering, and seeing the table properly covered, and things economically used, &c., &c."

Despite the assistance she received from others, however, Mrs. Washington's employments and duties were many and important; and it was only by habitually systematizing all her arrangements and occupations, that she was enabled to accomplish a personal superintendence of the various engagements of each successive day.

Continuing to rise, invariably, with the sun, as had always been her habit, she industriously devoted several hours to her domestic affairs, thus securing leisure for social enjoyments, and for attention to other avocations, without the neglect of household duties.

In the well-regulated mind of this disciplined and exemplary woman, each detail of daily life and habit found suitable attention. This was true even with reference to the exquisite neatness of her dress, which, though always entirely simple, was regarded as a model of refinement and propriety by her female friends. Carrying her keys at her side and making frequent visits to the various apartments connected with the elaborate arrangements of the table and its "aids and appliances," the spotless purity of her attire always remained unsullied by her active participation in the mysteries of each and all.

The direction and government of her servants, too, illustrated both the judgment and kindness of this admirable mistress. Prompt, regular, and industrious herself, she required like characteristics in those about her; but she tempered wholesome restraint by benevolent and sympathizing interest in whatever related to their collective or individual good; and, in addition to its many other attractions, the home of Mrs. Washington was celebrated for the superior excellence of its domestics.

It is recorded of this devout Christian, that never during her life, whether in prosperity or in adversity, did she omit that daily self-communion and self-examination, and those private devotional exercises, which would best prepare her for the self-control and self-denial by which she was, for more than half a century, so eminently distinguished. It was her habit to retire to her own apartment every morning after breakfast, there to devote an hour to solitary prayer and meditation.

Prominent among the multitudinous occupations of Mrs. Washington, were those connected with the varying but incessant requisitions of hospitality. She had always been remarked for the ease and elegance of her manners, and long practice in the graceful courtesies of the table had served to perfect her conversational powers; so that when again resuming these agreeable duties with her present advantages of place and position, she conducted the ceremonies of her ample and bountiful board with peculiar affability and self-possession, and led the conversation with singular felicity to subjects most congenial to the tastes, and familiar to the minds of all. Each varying theme was invested with attractiveness by her amiability and good sense; each guest seemed the object of her especial care and attention. And as her husband was habitually taciturn and abstracted, this happy tact, and this gentle womanly politeness, were particularly appropriate and necessary on the part of the hostess of Mount Vernon.

It will readily be supposed that retirement and solitude were unknown to the inmates of the *Home of* WASHINGTON.

It was the pleasure of the now rusticated American Commander-in-Chief and of "Lady Washington" to repay with grateful interest, those tokens of friendship and politeness which had been exhibited towards them, when both were, in some degree, the tests of unaffected and disinterested report and regard.

Her valued female friends,—the heroic compeers of "Lady Washington" through long, dark years of struggle and suffering,—renewed their intercourse with her under auspices most pleasing to all parties. The venerated members of the first Congress; the illustrious and time-honored Cincinnati; Washington's beloved companions in arms,—the faithful, though humble veterans of the well-fought fields of the Revolution; old friends and new; relations, connections and acquaintances, all "came trooping" to this shrine of Patriotism and Worth.

No distinguished foreigner who visited the new Land of Freedom, thought his tour complete without its including a pilgrimage to the home of the illustrious modern Cincinnatus. Many sought counsel and aid at his hands in the prosecution of objects of business, pleasure or philanthropy. Illustrative of this fact, there may be found among Washington's published Letters, together with many others of a similar nature, several addressed about this time to the celebrated Catharine Maccauley Graham; who, during a prolonged visit at Mount Vernon, endeavored to secure the interest of her host in her benevolent, though somewhat Utopian schemes of usefulness, and with whom he politely continued, subsequently, for some time to correspond.

But among the numerous guests who, during this period of Mrs. Washington's life, claimed the hospitalities of Mount Vernon, there were few whose arrival was anticipated with more pleasure, or whose welcome was more heart-felt, than that of the Marquis de La Fayette. There was, at one time, a hope entertained by his American friends, that this celebrated Champion of Liberty would be accompanied by the Marchioness in his visit to this country soon after the termination of the War in which he had borne so conspicuous a part. With this distinguished lady Mrs. Washington maintained the most cordial and pleasing correspondence, upon that, and kindred topics.—Nothing could surpass the affectionate veneration with which both these amiable foreigners regarded their beloved "Hero." Their eldest son and daughter bore, severally, the names of Washington and of his native State; and they long cherished the hope that he would, eventually, be enabled to fulfil a half-promise to visit France with Mrs. Washington. The succeeding passage from one of Washington's Letters to Madame de La Fayette, will furnish the reasons that were deemed sufficient to prevent the gratification of this hospitable wish, and exemplify the cordiality with which the Marchioness was invited to Mount Vernon.

"Mrs. Washington is highly honored by your participations, and feels very sensibly the force of your polite invitation to Paris; but she is too far advanced in life, and too much interested in the care of her little progeny to cross the Atlantic. This, my dear Marchioness, (indulge the freedom,) is not the case with you. You have youth (and if you should not incline to bring your children, can leave them with all the advantages of education,) and must have a curiosity to see the country, young, rude, and uncultivated as it is, for the liberties of which your husband has fought, bled, and acquired much glory, where everybody admires, everybody loves him. Come, then, let me entreat you, and call my cottage your home; for your own doors do not open to you with more readiness than mine would. You will see the plain manner in which we live, and meet with rustic civility, and you shall taste the simplicity of rural life. It will diversify the scene, and may give a higher relish for the gayeties of the court, when you return to Versailles. In these wishes, and in most respectful compliments, Mrs. Washington joins me. With sentiments of strong attachment, and very great regard, I have the honor to be, madam, &c."*

* In our inability to present our readers with specimens of Mrs. Washington's letters to this interesting family, we venture to commend to their perusal two selections from those ad-

In the mean while La Fayette returned, temporarily, to the country of his adoption, though without the Marchioness; and upon his arrival hastened directly to the presence of his dearest American friends. He passed a long-remembered fortnight of such happiness as rarely falls to the lot of mortals with his almost parental host and hostess at Mount Vernon, before commencing his general tour to the North, and returned again for another week of delightful intercourse with them, before his departure for his native land.

Nor was it by those alone who were so fortunate as to be able personally to pay their respects to Mrs. Washington, that she was gratefully and affectionately remembered long after she ceased to spend a portion of each year in intimate association with the martial companions of the Republican Commander-in-Chief. Thus, we find proofs of the kindly recollections ever cherished for her by the Count de Rochambeau; and records of the complimentary and oft-recurring messages of regard exchanged with him through her

dressed, about this time, by Washington to Madame De La Fayette, in which he represents himself as expressing the wishes and sentiments of both Mrs. Washington and himself. See NOTE C, of the Appendix.

husband. So, too, with Gen. Knox and innumerable others of their mutual friends.

We frequently discover traces of the prolonged continuance of much pleasing and friendly epistolary intercourse not only with these gentlemen, but with the ladies of their several families—of an interchange of the most cordial invitations, messages, &c., &c. Indeed the "Miscellaneous Correspondence" of Washington abounds with these incidental testimonials to the high appreciation entertained by her friends of the many and exalted excellencies of this celebrated lady, as well as with unequivocal manifestations of the unchanging interest and affection with which her husband constantly associated her with himself in all the various enjoyments and courtesies of social and domestic life.*

But agreeable and engrossing as were the engagements and enjoyments we have attempted faintly to delineate, they were far from occupying the attention of either Mrs. Washington or her husband to the exclusion of more important moral obligations.

* We are constrained to refer to the *Letters of Washington* for proofs and illustrations of our statements in relation to this interesting subject, because little of the correspondence of Mrs. Washington is extant, or at least, attainable for publication.

After the nine years of Washington's unbroken absence, and of the very frequent and protracted departures of Mrs. Washington from home, and in the unsettled state of all private as well as public affairs, it is not remarkable that both should deem it important, for the sake of those dependent upon them, if not for their own personal advantage, that strict order and method should be instituted in all matters appertaining to individual and household expenditure. But whatever necessity arose for curtailment in the pecuniary arrangements of this truly conscientious and estimable pair, was made to fall, not upon their benevolent and charitable resources, but upon their powers of self-denial in matters of luxurious indulgence or personal convenience. Thus, though Washington at one time uncompromisingly countermanded an order for silver plate previously given, through the Marquis de La Fayette to his Parisian agents, when he thought, upon a further investigation of his affairs, that he could not conveniently meet the necessary expense and continue his other outlays, he, about the same time, gave the sum of £1000 to the Academy at Alexandria, and made the most kind and generous provision for an unfortunate connection who sought his aid. He, also, during many years, "gave fifty pounds annually for the instruction of indigent children in Alexandria; and by will he left a legacy of four thousand dol lars, the net income of which was to be used for the same benevolent object forever."

To obligations like these, and to objects and designs of a similar nature, all considerations of less moral importance were systematically and habitually made subservient. United in the most faithful, cheerful, and enlightened regard for the requisitions of philanthropy, the necessities of dependants and the promptings of beneficence, these congenial and exalted spirits found more genuine gratification in the unobtrusive charities that marked their mutual career, than all the pomp and luxury of a regal establishment could have yielded them.

Meanwhile the progress of national events—so important, so interesting to all—engaged a share of the attention of one long and intimately connected with the most prominent actors in the affairs of her country.

Mrs. Washington partook her husband's high pleasure in the early adoption of the Federal Constitution by her native State; and, though now seldom tempted to leave home, probably participated with him in the public festivities by which their friends in the city of Alexandria were the first to celebrate an occurrence so gratifying to the Patriot of Mount Vernon; who thus briefly alludes to the expressive rejoicings elicited by the occasion, in a letter written immediately after his return home:—"The citizens of Alexandria when convened constituted the first public company in America, which had the pleasure of pouring a libation to the prosperity of the ten States that had actually adopted the General Government."*

Mrs. Washington was too true-hearted a daughter of the "Old Dominion," and too enlightened in her patriotism and philanthropy, not greatly to rejoice in the gradual development of the auspicious events by which the general good, not of her native country alone, but of the whole civilized world, was destined to be so essentially and enduringly promoted.

Though now considerably past fifty years of age, and becoming somewhat portly in person, Mrs. Washington's rational, healthful habits, and the ceaseless influence of the principles by which her life was habitually regulated, enabled her still

* Letter to C. C. Pinkney, Esq., Mount Vernon, June 28, 1788.

to exhibit undiminished her characteristic activity, usefulness and cheerfulness. As a wife, a parent, a mistress, a hostess, and a friend, she was equally admirable, and a happy combination of the best qualities of each and all! In short, Mrs. Washington was at this time, in manner, appearance, and character, the pleasing and graceful representative of a class of which the model is now, unfortunately, lost—a *Lady of the Olden Time!* "She appeared to me," recorded an admiring visitor* who was, in the absence of her husband, the guest of Mrs. Washington during the period to which our narrative at present relates, "one of the best women in the world, and beloved by all about her. She * * * * was surrounded by her grand-children and Mrs. Custis, her son's widow."

The fairy forms and playful sports of the youthful inmates alluded to in this brief but expressive eulogium, were long the admiration of every visitor at Mount Vernon, as they were the pride and delight of its amiable mistress, whose judicious advice and assistance materially aided their mother in conducting their education. Deeply impressed with the importance of this grateful

* The Marquis de Chastellux.

task, Mrs. Washington regularly devoted much time and attention to these favored recipients of her love and care, and her husband formally adopted one of the three little daughters of Mrs. Custis as his own.

With this general and imperfect description of the peaceful and congenial pleasures and employments of a delightful and fleeting portion of the existence of our heroine,—a period replete with exemplifications of the happy fate we have before ascribed to her, that of being ever surrounded by a glowing halo of affection,—we release our readers from further attention to this portion of our subject.

CHAPTER IX.

Must I thus leave thee, Paradise? Thus leave
Thee, native soil, these happy walks and shades
Fit haunt of gods? MILTON.

The World is with me, and its many cares,
Its woes—its wants—the anxious hopes and fears
That wait on all terrestrial affairs—
The shades of former and of future years—
Foreboding fancies, and prophetic tears,
Quelling a spirit that was once elate. HOOD.

THE time too soon arrived when his ever-sacred duty to his country compelled the illustrious Farmer of Mount Vernon to peril his mental and domestic peace, as he had formerly done his "life, his fortune, and his sacred honor," by leaving the delightful retreat in which he had earnestly hoped to secure future exemption from the burdensome public duties to which he had devoted so large a portion of his past life.

Mrs. Washington's reluctance to leave, for gayer and more ceremonious scenes, the quiet pleasures and congenial pursuits from which she derived so much gratification, as well as her sentiments in relation to other equally interesting subjects, will be most satisfactorily learned from a Letter addressed by her, soon after her arrival at the Seat of Government, to an old and confidential friend :—

MRS. WASHINGTON TO MRS. WARREN.

"Your very friendly letter of last month has afforded me much more satisfaction, than all the formal compliments and empty ceremonies of mere etiquette could possibly have done. I am not apt to forget the feelings which have been inspired by my former society with good acquaintances, nor to be insensible to their expressions of gratitude to the President; for you know me well enough to do me the justice to believe, that I am fond only of what comes from the heart. Under a conviction that the demonstrations of respect and affection to him originate in that source, I cannot deny, that I have taken some interest and pleasure in them. The difficulties which presented themselves to view upon his first entering upon the Presidency, seem thus to be in some measure surmounted. It is owing to the kindness of our numerous friends in all quarters, that my new and unwished-for situation is not indeed a burden to me. When I was much younger, I should probably have enjoyed the innocent gayeties of life as much as most persons of my age; but I had long since placed all the prospects of my future worldly happiness in the still enjoyments of the fireside at Mount Vernon.

"I little thought when the war was finished, that any circumstances could possibly happen, which would call the General into public life again. I had anticipated, that from that moment we should be suffered to grow old together in solitude and tranquillity. That was the first and dearest wish of my heart. I will not, however, contemplate with too much regret, disappointments that were inevitable, though his feelings and my own were in perfect unison with respect to our predilection for private life, yet I cannot blame him for having acted according to his ideas of duty in obeying the voice of his country. The consciousness of having attempted to do all the good in his power, and the pleasure of finding his fellow-citizens so well satisfied with the disinterestedness of his conduct, will doubtless be some compensation for the great sacrifices which I know he has made. Indeed, on his journey from Mount Vernon to this place, in his late tour through the Eastern States, by every public and every private information which has come to him, I am persuaded he has experienced nothing to make him repent his having acted from what he conceives to be a sense of indispensable duty. On the contrary, all his sensibility has been awakened in receiving such repeated and unequivocal proofs of sincere regard from his countrymen.

"With respect to myself, I sometimes think the arrangement is not quite as it ought to have been, that I, who had much rather be at home, should occupy a place, with which a great many younger and gayer women would be extremely pleased. As my grand-children and domestic connections make up a great portion of the felicity which I looked for in this world, I shall hardly be able to find any substitute, that will indemnify me for the loss of such endearing society. I do not say this because I feel dissatisfied with my present station, for everybody and everything conspire to make me as contented as possible in it; yet I have learned too much of the vanity of human affairs to expect felicity from the scenes of public life. I am still determined to be cheerful and happy in whatever situation I may be; for I have also learned from experience, that the greater part of our happiness or misery depends on our dispositions, and not on our circumstances. We carry the seeds of the one or the other about with us in our minds, wherever we go.

I have two of my grand-children with me, who enjoy advantages in point of education, and who, I trust, by the goodness of Providence, will be a great blessing to me. My other two grand-children are with their mother in Virginia."—New York, December 26th, 1789.*

The subjoined passage from Mrs. Warren's reply to this highly engaging and expressive communication, truly indicates, as she herself intimates, the feelings of the numerous friends of the wife of the first President:—

"Your observation may be true, that many younger and gayer ladies consider your situation as enviable; yet I know not one, who, by general consent, would be more likely to obtain the suffrages of the sex, even were they to canvass at election, for this elevated station, than the lady who now holds the first rank in the United States."

* Published by Mr. Sparks from the *Original MS.*

Our readers will not have failed to remark the unostentatious allusion contained in Mrs. Washington's Letter, to the scenes and adventures of the journey of the President elect from Mount Vernon to New York;* and all will remember the peculiar incidents of that triumphal progress—unrivalled as it is in the lives of the Kings and Conquerors of the World!

Every generous heart will beat in unison with the delightful emotions that must have glowed in the bosom of the Patriot Wife while witnessing the spontaneous manifestations of enthusiastic gratitude and reverence with which the immortal SAVIOUR OF HIS COUNTRY was everywhere hailed, from the time of his departure from home to the auspicious hour of his imposing and august inauguration. The glorious ceremonial at the Bridge of Trenton has no parallel in all history for its deep

* Some of our readers may have forgotten that the first organization of the Federal Government (April, 1789) took place at New York. Philadelphia was afterwards the seat of the General Government. It was not until the year 1791 that the present location was selected by WASHINGTON, to whom that duty was formally delegated by his countrymen. Thus, then, Mrs. Washington passed the first year of the Presidency of her husband at New York, the second at Philadelphia, and the remaining six at the present National Capitol.

pathos and moral sublimity. It drew tears even from eyes "unused to the melting mood"—those of the imperturbable "*Defender of the Mothers*" and "*Protector of the Daughters*" of America.

Words poorly avail to tell the pure and exalted happiness of the WIFE OF WASHINGTON, when participating with him in joys so little alloyed by the dross of earth! In pleasures like these she received a high remuneration for the sacrifice of personal tastes and wishes involved in her change of residence and position.

We behold this estimable, exemplary, and gifted woman assuming the obligations and responsibilities of her novel and exalted station, with the same ease and grace, the same self-possession and serenity, the same ready self-adaptation and feminine tact that had distinguished her in every previous phase of her varied and eventful career.

When deciding, for the first time, upon the external manifestations, so to speak, of public order and system, the authority of law and the reality of National Independence, policy and propriety equally demanded that the visible tokens of each should be sufficiently imposing to impress the popular mind and exact respect from all observers.

Hence the prominence given to the mere insignia and appendages of power.

In accordance with this judicious design, the Mansion of the First President of the new Republic was furnished with stately elegance, and the daily routine of its arrangements was conducted with much more elaborate observance of the requisitions of courtly etiquette than is now required either by popular taste or political necessity.*

* The principal servants connected with the Presidential establishment wore the family livery—white with red collars and cuffs. The chariot in which President Washington performed his celebrated tour through the United States, was also *white*. This was probably the color of the carriage in which Mrs. Washington made visits of ceremony in New York and Philadelphia. The *horses* of the President were noted for their great beauty and value. Those used by Mrs. Washington were *bays*. The chief domestics of the household were a steward, housekeeper, porter, coachman, and cook. The former and latter were personages distinguished by family tradition. *Francis* the steward, wore, when in his official post at the sideboard, during the state dinners, silk small clothes, white silk stockings, and his hair elaborately dressed and powdered! It was the pride and business of his life to contribute his full share towards sustaining the dignity and consequence of the family he had the honor to serve, through the most ostentatious displays permitted by the restraining supervision of his methodical and judicious master. *Hercules*, the colored cook, was one of the

The Levees of Mrs. Washington were held on Friday evening of each week; those of the President on each Tuesday, from three to four o'clock. The "Congressional dinners" occurred on Thursday.

The company, on the occasion of Mrs. Washington's Levees, assembled at an early hour, and usually retired at a little past ten.* The ladies were seated, and the President was accustoned to address some appropriate remarks to each, in turn, as he passed round the circle. At these drawing-rooms, Mrs. Robert Morris always occupied the seat at the right hand of the Lady of the Mansion.

We have no means of describing the dress worn by Mrs. Washington during her receptions;

most finished and renowned dandies of the age in which he flourished, as well as a highly accomplished adept in the mysteries of the important art he so long and so diligently practised.

* The author remembers to have somewhere read, (though upon what authority the statement was based, she cannot now reçall,) that, as the usual hour of separation drew near, the expressive air of "Home, sweet Home," not unfrequently saluted the ears of the assemblage; and that Mrs. Washington was wont sometimes quietly to remark that the General retired at half-past ten!

but we know that the etiquette of the day required that all gentlemen who attended the drawing-rooms of the National Chief Magistrate should appear in full *full dress;* and we infer that there was not less ceremony observed by both ladies and gentlemen at the Levees of Mrs. Washington. The costume of the President at his own Levees, (and probably at those of Mrs. Washington also,) was a black velvet coat and small clothes, with a dress sword, a *chapeau de bras* adorned with a cockade and fringed with short black feathers, knee and shoe buckles, and orange-colored gloves; his hair, of course, powdered, and "gathered behind in a silk bag." There were no seats in the apartment where the President stood, with his Secretaries and other attendants, to receive his guests on these State Days. Visitors advanced in succession, paid their respects to the Head of the Republic, and were addressed by him in return; but the President offered his hand to no one.

At all dinners given by the Republican Chief Magistrate, the venerable Robert Morris took precedence of every other guest, invariably conducted Mrs. Washington, and sat at her right hand.

"On the great National festivals of the Fourth of July and Twenty-second of February, the sages of the Revolutionary Congress and the officers of the Revolutionary Army renewed their acquaintance with Mrs. Washington; many and kindly greetings took place, with many a recollection of the days of trial. The Cincinnati, after paying their respects to their Chief, were seen to file off towards the parlor, where "Lady Washington" was in waiting to receive them, and where Wayne, and Mifflin, and Dickenson, and Stewart, and Moylan, and Hartley, and a host of veterans, were cordially welcomed as old friends, and where many an interesting reminiscence was called up, of the head-quarters and the "times of the Revolution."

On the National fête days, the commencement of the Levee was announced by the firing of a salute from a pair of twelve-pounders, stationed not far distant from the Presidential Mansion; and the ex-Commander-in-Chief paid his former companions in arms the compliment to wear the old Continental uniform.

It was customary for the gentlemen officially connected with the family of the President to receive the ladies who came to pay their respects to Mrs. Washington, attend them from their carriages to her presence; but Washington himself performed that service when the venerated widows of the beloved and lamented Greene and Montgomery called at the Presidential Mansion.

Visitors were not received either by the President or Mrs. Washington on the Sabbath. They habitually attended divine service during the day, and in the evening her husband read from the Bible, or some other devotional book, to Mrs. Washington in her own apartment.

"There was one description of visitors, however, to be found about the first President's Mansion on all days. The old soldiers repaired, as they said, to head-quarters, just to inquire after the health of his Excellency and Lady Washington. They knew his Excellency was, of course, much engaged; but they would like to see the good lady. One had been a soldier of the Life Guard; another had been on duty when the British threatened to surprise the head-quarters; a third had witnessed that terrible fellow, Cornwallis, surrender his sword; each one had some touching appeal, with which he introduced himself to the peaceful head-quarters of the presidoliad. All were "kindly bid to stay," were conducted to the steward's apartments, and refreshments set before them; and after receiving some little token from the lady, with her best wishes for the health and happiness of an old soldier, they went their ways, while blessings upon their revered Commander and the good Lady Washington, were uttered by many a war-worn veteran of the Revolution."*

In her new and interesting position as the wife of the first President of the American Republic, Mrs. Washington continued to be distinguished by the quiet good breeding, dignified simplicity, self-possession, and equanimity for which she had long been remarkable. She received the respect, the compliments, and the honors rendered to her high station without the assumption of undue self-importance, and without the affectation of inappropriate humility. She presided at her elegant and bountiful table with the same courteous ease and kindly affability that formerly shed an almost

* Perhaps some of our readers may be disposed to ascribe *puerility* to the minuteness of our details in relation to the peculiarities of Mrs. Washington's present mode of life. The author hopes, nevertheless, to afford passing entertainment to others whose taste for antiquarian research may be, perhaps, in some degree gratified.

inimitable charm over the hospitalities of Mount Vernon; and continued, as before, to lead the conversation on such occasions, to subjects suited to the innocent conviviality of the hour.*

Her beloved grand-children continued to engage the affections and enjoy the society and attention of Mrs. Washington, not only when she was comparatively at leisure in the retirement of Mount Vernon, but when residing at the seat of Government, and involved in the formal routine of public life. The eldest of this little band were now rapidly becoming interesting social companions for the paternal guide to whom they were so much indebted.

* Mrs. Washington possessed too much natural good sense and too clear a conception of propriety to converse publicly upon subjects involving her husband's political interests or official policy. Foreign ambassadors and strangers frequently attempted to draw her into a discussion of political topics; but it was her invariable practice to waive all discourse of this nature. —But, though it had never, during her long public career, been the habit of Mrs. W. to give open expression to her political sentiments, no want of independence withheld their manifestation when circumstances required their promulgation. In the year 1780 an *Address* was published in the Philadelphia newspapers, entitled, "*The Sentiments of an American Woman*," which was attributed to her, and which was publicly read in the Churches throughout Virginia.

This disinterested friend did not, however, avail herself of the opportunities afforded by her exalted position to secure either personal aggrandizement, or the exclusive benefit of her own family. The daughters of her old and well-remembered Revolutionary companions, shared with her grand-children in the high social advantages it was now in her power to afford them; and all to whom she was bound by the cherished ties of former years, received the most convincing proofs of the perpetuity of a friendship that was ever equally thoughtful, active, and sincere, whether engendered by the clinging tendencies of a youthful heart, fostered amid the snow-thatched hovels of Valley Forge, enshrined beneath the hospitable roof of Mount Vernon, or lending interest, grace, and warmth to the stately courtesies of the National Capital!

During each year of the double Presidential term of office, Mrs. Washington returned for at least a portion of the summer, to Mount Vernon. Indeed the health of her husband, impaired by his too arduous labors, soon imperatively required that temporary exemption from bodily fatigue and mental exertion, which he could there alone secure, as well as the watchful care she could so judiciously and affectionately bestow.

There is no record of Mrs. Washington's having accompanied the President in his journey to New England, during the year following that of his election to the Chief Magistracy; nor of her being the companion of his long and well-known tour in the year 1791. We, therefore, infer that she preferred the repose and seclusion which she could best enjoy in her favorite retreat, surrounded by the household companions who might almost be said to impersonate the *Penates* of Mount Vernon.

Devoted to the varied and important duties of her high station, eight successive years sped away in pleasures and occupations, which, if not those most congenial to the conjugal, maternal, and domestic tastes and affections of this eminent American Matron, were yet crowned by the grateful consciousness of usefulness, and the high approbation of that mental guide, to the test of whose scrutinizing arbitration she was wont to submit each thought, word, and action of her life.

The final departure of President and Mrs. Washington from the place and power through which they had acquired so much personal honor, and conferred such lasting benefit upon their country, was distinguished by every manifestation of national and individual reverence and gratitude.

All mourned the retirement of the great and good Father of his Country, from the immediate supervision to which all might so safely and implicitly trust; and the love and blessings of a nation followed both Mrs. Washington and its honored Chief to the well-earned tranquillity of private life.

Many were the tender farewells of those who were to be forever officially separated, and many the parting tokens of remembrance and affection long preserved as the sacred mementoes of those patriarchal days.

Mrs. Washington's part in these touching adieux will be characteristically illustrated by the following pleasing anecdote, for which we are obliged to a gentleman who personally received it from the most authentic source :—

"On leaving the Seat of Government after the inauguration of his successor, Washington presented to all his principal officers some token of regard. When Mrs. Oliver Wolcott, the wife of one of these gentlemen, and the particular friend and correspondent of Miss Custis, called 'to take leave,' Mrs. Washington asked if she did not wish a memorial of the General. 'Yes,' replied Mrs. Wolcott, 'I should like a lock of his hair.' Mrs. Washington instantly took her scissors, and with a happy smile, cut a large lock from her husband's head, added to it one from her own, and presented them to her fair friend."

"Nor place, nor titles, made Aspasia's bliss;
* * * * * *
Unmoved she saw the glittering trifles perish,
And thought the petty dross beneath a sigh.
Cheerful she followed to the rural cell;
Love for her wealth, and her distinction *Virtue!*"

CHAPTER X.

And a vision of happiness steals through
her rest— **Dimond.**

Cease, then, the funeral strain!—Lament no more,
Whom, rife for fate, 'twere impious to deplore!
He died the death of glory. Cease to mourn,
And cries of grief to songs of triumph turn!
Ah, no!—Awhile, ere reason's voice o'erpowers
The fond regret that weeps a loss like ours,
* * * * * *
Yet, yet awhile, the natural tear may flow,
Nor cold reflection chide the chastening woe! **Scott.**

Yes, there *is* pain in this
Most passionate longing to o'erreach the clay—
This exile-thirst, which stronger grows each day
To take the morning-wings and flee away
To realms of future bliss. **Mrs. E. J. Eames.**

Relieved, at last, from the irksomeness of elaborate ceremony, and the time-engrossing duties of a public station, the illustrious Subject of our Memoir returned permanently, in the Spring of 1797, to the earnestly-coveted and peaceful enjoyments of the home from which she had so often and so long been exiled.

Never had that home seemed so worthy to be graced by the continued presence of its gentle and admirable mistress. The walks, the gardens, the grounds, the venerable mansion, all gave most pleasing token of the refined taste and careful supervision of the beneficent spirits who shed everywhere around them so benign an influence.

But, though the effects of their previous efforts were so plainly discernible, General and Mrs. Washington entered, with much zeal and interest, upon projects for the further improvement and embellishment of the intended asylum of their declining years.

And now these faithful votaries of nature, these unaffected lovers of all the thousand nameless joys that constitute the sacred charm of HOME, contemplated with exquisite pleasure the calm vista through which they could at last trace their mutual pathway along the vale of time. A temperate enjoyment of the luxuries afforded by affluence, the affectionate reverence of dependants and relations, the exalted pleasures of friendship, the heavenly delights of benevolence, the joys of conjugal love—all these sources of happiness were theirs!

> "And memory stood sidewise, half covered with flowers,
> Displaying each rose, but secreting its thorn,"

while recalling the many varying incidents of

long years of high duty and successful effort, of well-rewarded self-sacrifice and eventual triumph!

Such were the natural and appropriate rewards that crowned a life so useful, so virtuous, so exalted as that which it has been our desire to sketch in these brief pages! Unfettered by the "irons of circumstance," through each changing scene of her eventful career, Mrs. Washington had been faithful to the dictates of a noble nature, disciplined and controlled by Christian principle. Yielding to no selfish, effeminate love of the *dolce far niente* of existence, nor yet to the insidious promptings of worldly ambition, but ever "true to the kindred points of Heaven and Home," she had passed unfalteringly on, scathed neither by the fierce lightnings of adversity, nor the dazzling splendor of place and power. The wordless eloquence expressed by the serene majesty of her life, commends itself to our hearts with far more resistless pathos than all the eulogies panegyrists could pronounce, or poet's pen; and we turn from the contemplation of her character with mingled emotions of admiration, affection, and humility!

Felicity such as now blessed the venerable mistress of Mount Vernon partook too little of the usual attributes of human happiness to be perpetuated on earth.

Two years after his final resignation of the cares of state, the immortal Washington was suddenly summoned to possess, in the revealed presence of Deity,

"Through boundless Space and countless Time,"

the immutable bliss of a "*just man made perfect!*"

Mrs. Washington never for a moment left the apartment of her husband during the brief and severe illness that terminated his existence. Kneeling by his bedside, she bowed her throbbing brow upon the sacred records of those Holy Promises and Consolations that could alone sustain her spirit in this the hour of her most agonizing trial.

"The last effort of the expiring Washington was worthy of the Roman fame of his life and character. He raised himself up, and casting a look of benignity on all around him, as if to thank them for their kindly attentions, he composed his limbs, closed his eyes, and folding his arms upon his bosom, the Father of his Country expired, gently as though an infant died!" "Favored of Heaven, he departed without exhibiting the weakness of humanity; magnanimous in death, the darkness of the grave could not obscure his brightness!"

Fate had now dealt the last deadly blow to the earthly happiness of Mrs. Washington! Her children, their father, the faithful, affectionate, sympathizing friend and counsellor, with whom, through unnumbered years, she had stood side by side in many and grievous trials, dangers, and sorrows,—all were gone! The desolate survivor stood like a lone sentinel upon a deserted battle-field, regarding in mute despair the fatal destruction of hope, and love, and joy!

> "She sheds no tears, her grief's too highly wrought:
> 'Tis speechless agony!"

Long did the heart-stricken mourner linger amid the familiar objects that, like the faces of old friends, everywhere met her sorrowful eyes, and in the beloved presence of all that was mortal of the august Christian Philosopher, to whose memory the apartment where he reposed would be forever consecrated. Yielding at last to the entreaties of affection, she turned a long, soul-harrowing gaze upon the placid features of the mighty dead, and then departing from these hallowed precincts, never more returned to a spot replete with associations at once sorrowful and inviolate!

The shock occasioned by the intelligence of the death of WASHINGTON "fell upon the country with the unexpected suddenness of an earthquake; dismay and affliction suspended all business; all ages and classes united in demonstrations of respect and affection."

"By an arrangement with the Government, Mrs. Washington yielded the remains of the Chief to the prayers of the nation, as expressed through its representatives in Congress, conditioning that, at her decease, her own remains should accompany those of her husband to the Capital. The earthly relics of the great PATER PATRIÆ were then consigned to the Family Tomb within the grounds of Mount Vernon, there to await the final disposition of his country."*

"When the burst of grief which followed the death of the *Pater Patriæ* had a little subsided, visits of condolence to the bereaved lady were

* NATIONAL PORTRAIT GALLERY.

made by the first personages of the land. The President of the United States, with many other distinguished individuals, repaired to Mount Vernon, while letters,* addresses, funeral orations, and all the tokens of sorrow and respect, loaded the mails from every quarter of the country, offering the sublime tribute of a nation's mourning for a nation's benefactor."†

But grateful and consolatory as were these spontaneous manifestations of reverential regard for the memory of her illustrious husband, Mrs. Washington possessed a far higher and dearer source of confidence in his eternal happiness than any earthly fiat could bestow, in her inward and assured conviction that he had ever sought the same "*fountain of living waters*," from which she had herself drunk deep of heavenly hope and joy !‡

* A letter addressed to Mrs. Washington on this solemn occasion by the *Earl of Bucan*, the brother of Lord Erskine, and the distant relative of Washington, has recently been discovered among the papers of Mrs. W., by her grand-daughter, Mrs. Lawrence Lewis, and given to the public. Our readers will not be displeased with its insertion in this volume, though it is characterized by some peculiarities of style and expression. See NOTE D, of the Appendix.

† NATIONAL PORTRAIT GALLERY.

‡ We present our readers with a communication upon this

The venerable Subject of our Memoir now looked eagerly and intently forward to the termination of that journey in which she had been preceded by all who were most dear to her. Devoutly resting her wounded spirit upon the soothing conviction that those from whom she was here separated would then be forever restored to her, she strengthened herself to tread on in the weary way of life, with mournful but unshaken confidence in the blessed truth that "all things work together for good" in the orderings of the Great Disposer of events. Hers was was not the callousness of indifference or insensibility, the obtuseness of a benighted stoicism, or the lightness of a shallow intellect; but the undoubting constancy of a Christian, whose faith in Him who

"—— giveth, with paternal care,
Howe'er unjustly we complain,
To each their necessary share
Of joy and sorrow, health and pain,"

---

highly interesting subject, addressed, at his request, to Mr. Sparks, by the adopted daughter of Washington, Miss Custis, who was twenty years an inmate of the family of her kind protector. Any attempt to abridge these agreeably-written paragraphs must, necessarily, diminish the pleasing simplicity and frankness that lend additional interest to the details they contain.—See Note E, of the Appendix.

no mortal suffering could disturb, no sublunary occurrence could destroy!

But neither her changeless grief, nor her deep interest in the concerns of a future state of existence, were regarded by this exemplary and self-sacrificing Christian as entitling her to exemption from vigilant attention to the requisitions of actual and practical life. The many cares assumed by the helpful, judicious, kindly friend who had formerly shared her toils and duties, now rested solely upon her. Yet though Mrs. Washington was in her sixty-ninth year, she still conducted the various affairs of her extensive establishment with her previous diligence, regularity, and skill, and discharged the numerous obligations of the hostess of Mount Vernon, with wonted dignity and urbanity. More grave, more silent, she might be; but no duty was forgotten or omitted in relation to domestic arrangements, no courtesy neglected towards the innumerable votaries who sought, in sorrowing pilgrimage, Columbia's more than Mecca-shrine.

> "Light grief is fond of state and courts compassion,
> But there's a dignity in cureless sorrow,
> A sullen grandeur, which disdains complaint.

Yet, despite this outward composure, this habitual self-control, this hospitable amenity, her lustreless and abstracted eye, and the one glowing spot in her else blanched and faded cheek, betrayed only too plainly the ceaseless struggle of that noble spirit!

> "She lived—for life may long be borne
> Ere sorrow break its chain!"

But what was earth, what was life, to this bereaved and heart-stricken mourner!

Thus passed two long years for the worn and weary earth-wanderer; and then her sudden and serious illness spread consternation to the outermost circle of the many loving and sympathizing hearts that ever environed her.

Dr. Craik, the old and highly-esteemed physician of the family, well aware of the insidious mental foe that had but too surely undermined the strength of his patient, scarce spoke of hope to the sorrowing household, and Mrs. Washington was herself aware of her approaching dissolution.

Dying as she had lived, mindful of duty to the last, the expiring Christian summoned the several members of her family to attend her death-bed, and addressed to her grand-children, particularly, the most solemn and impressive words of exhortation and advice. She bore the most unequivocal and triumphant testimony to her unwavering reliance upon the hopes and assurances of the Religion that had been the guide and support of her long and varied life, and with that appropriate and pathetic farewell, this celebrated American Matron tranquilly rendered back her earthly existence to Him from whom it was received.

The death of Mrs. Washington occurred in the year 1801, and during the seventy-first year of her age.

Her remains, in accordance with her desire, were enclosed in a leaden coffin, and placed beside those of Washington in the family tomb at Mount Vernon.

APPENDIX

TO

MARTHA WASHINGTON.

APPENDIX TO MARTHA WASHINGTON.

NOTE A.

Mr. Sparks gives us the original List, as found among Washington's papers. For explanatory particulars, see Sparks' Life of Washington, Vol. II. 329. We, of course, copy *exactly*, from Mr. S.

" A Salmon-colored Tabby of the enclosed pattern, with satin flowers, to be made in a sack and coat. One Cap, Handkerchief, Tucker, and Ruffles to be made of Brussels lace, or point, proper to wear with the above negligee, to cost £20 One piece Bag Holland at 6s. (a yard.) 2 fine flowered Lawn Aprons. 2 double Handkerchiefs. 1 pair woman's white Silk Hose. 6 pairs fine Cotton do. 4 pairs Thread do. 1 pair black and 1 pair white Satin Shoes, of the smallest 5s. 4 pairs Calamanco, do. 1 fashionable Hat, or

Bonnet. 6 pairs woman's best Kid Gloves. 8 pairs ditto mits. 1-2 dozen Knots and Breast Knots. 1 doz. round Silk laces. 1 black Mask. 1 doz. most fashionable Pocket Handkerchiefs. 2 pairs neat, small Scissors. 1 lb. sewing silk, shaded. 4 pieces binding Tape. 6 m. Minikin Pins. 1 m. Hair ditto. 6 lbs. perfumed Powder. 3 lbs. best Scotch Snuff. 3 lbs. best violette Strasburg. 8 lbs. Starch. 2 lbs. powdered Blue. 2 oz. Coventry Thread, one of which to be very fine. 1 piece narrow white satin Ribbon, pearl edge. 1 case of Pickles, to consist of Anchovies, Capers, Olives, Salad Oil, and 1 bottle India Mangoes. One large Cheshire Cheese. 4 lbs. Green Tea. 10 groce best corks. 25 lbs. best jar Raisins. 25 lbs. Almonds, in the shell 1 hogshead best Porter. 10 loaves double and 10 single refined sugar. * * * * * 12 lbs. best Mustard. 2 doz. Jack's playing Cards. * * * * * 1 1-2 doz. Bell glasses for Garden. 2 more Chair Bottoms, such as were written for in a former invoice. 1 more Windsor Curtain and Cornice. 100 lbs. White Biscuit. 3 gallons of Rhenish in bottles."

There then follows a long enumeration of articles, evidently designed for the use and comfort of the slaves upon the estate; among which we observe "350 yds. Kendall Cotton," "100 Dutch Blankets," &c., &c., together with numerous Garden, Carpenter's, and Farming tools, and articles of Cutlery and Iron-ware, sufficient to supply a colony preparing to populate a deserted island of considerable size!

Among the medicines ordered (and the list seems to us to include the whole *Materia Medica!*) we light upon the agreeable items of "Pearl Barley" and "Sago," "5 lbs. White Sugar Candy," "10 lbs. Brown do.," "1 lb. Barley Sugar."

After this follows an array of the names of medicines to be used in Farriery; and the whole is concluded by the following—

Invoice of Sundries to be shipped by Robert Cary and Company, for the use of Master John and Miss Patty Custis, each to be charged to their own accounts, but both consigned to George Washington, Potomac River.

For Master Custis, 6 *years old.*—1 piece Irish Holland, at 4s. 2 yards fine Cambric, at 10s. 6 pocket Handkerchiefs, small and fine. 6 pairs Gloves; 2 Laced Hats. 2 pieces India Nankeen. 6 pairs fine thread Stockings, 4 pairs coarser do. 4 pairs worsted do. 4 pairs strong Shoes; 4 pairs Pumps. 1 summer suit of clothes, to be made of something light and thin. 3 fine Ivory Combs; 2 Horn do., and 2 Brushes. 1 piece black Hair Ribbon. 1 pair handsome Silver Shoe and Knee Buckles. 10s. worth of Toys. 6 little books for children beginning to read. 1 oz. 8d. Thread; 1 oz. 12d. do.; 1 oz. 2s. do.; 1 oz. 3s. do. 1-2 lb. whited brown Thread. 1 light duffel Cloak with silver frogs.

For Miss Custis, 4 *years old.*—8 yards fine printed Linen, at 3s. 6d. 1 piece Irish Holland, at 4s. 2 ells fine Holland, at 10s. 8 pairs kid Mits; 4 pairs gloves. 2 pairs silk shoes. 4 pairs Calemanco do.; 4 pairs leather Pumps. 6 pairs fine thread Stockings. 4 pairs worsted do. 1-2 piece flowered Dimity. 2 yards fine Cambric, at 10s. 2 Caps, 2 pairs Ruffles, 2 Tuckers, Bibs, and Aprons, if fashionable. 2 Fans; 2 Masks; 2 Bonnets. 2 m. large Pins; 2 m. short whites; 2 m. Minikins; 1 Cloth Cloak. 1 stiffened Coat of Fashionable Silk, made to packthread stays. 6 yards Ribbon; 2 Necklaces. 1 pair Silver Sleeve Buttons, with stones. 1 fashionable-dressed baby, 10s.; and other Toys, 10s. 6 Pocket Handkerchiefs.

NOTE B.

"NOVEMBER 24th.—After dinner, as I had heard some threats thrown out, that if the ball assembled this night, as it was proposed, they presumed that the New Tavern would cut but a poor figure to-morrow morning, these fears of some commotion's being made that would be very disagreeable at this melancholy time, in disturbing the peace of the city, I concluded if possible, to prevent, in order to which I went to Colonel Hancock's lodgings, and finding he was not come from Congress, and the time grew short, being three o'clock, I walked up to the State House, in expectation of meeting him. That failing, I requested the door-keeper to call Samuel Adams, which he accordingly did, and he came. I then informed him of the account received of a ball, that was to be held this evening, and where, and that Mrs. Washington and Colonel Hancock's wife were to be present, and as such meetings appeared to be contrary to the Eighth Resolve of Congress, I therefore requested he would give my respects to

Colonel Hancock, desire him to wait on Lady Washington to request her not to attend or go this evening. This he promised. Thence I went and met the Committee at Philosophic Hall, which was large and respectable, being called together for this only purpose to consider the propriety of this meeting or ball's being held this evening in this city, at the New Tavern, where, after due and mature consideration, it was then concluded, there being but one dissenting voice, (Sharp Delany,) that there should be no such meeting held, not only this evening, but in future, while these troublesome times continued, and a Committee was appointed, immediately, to go and inform the directors of the meeting not to proceed any further in this affair, and also to wait upon Lady Washington, expressing this Committee's great regard and affection to her, requesting her to accept of their grateful acknowledgments and respect, due to her on account of her near connection with our worthy and brave General, now exposed in the field of battle in defence of our rights and liberties, and request and desire her not to grace that company, to which we are informed, she has an invitation this evening, &c., &c. Came home near six. After I drank coffee,

I went down to Samuel Adams' lodgings, where was Colonel Dyer. Spent some time pleasantly, until Colonel Harrison came to rebuke Samuel Adams for using his influence for the stoppage of this entertainment which he declared was legal, just and laudable. Many arguments were used by all present to convince him of the impropriety at this time, but all to no effect; so as he came out of humor, he so returned, to appearance.

"November 25th.—At half past eleven, went to the Committee Room at the Coffee House; came away near two. At this time Major Bayard, one of the four gentlemen appointed to wait on Lady Washington, reported that they had acted agreeably to directions, that the lady received them with great politeness, thanked the Committee for their kind care and regard in giving such timely notice, requesting her best compliments to be returned to them for their care and regard, and to assure them that their sentiments on this occasion, were perfectly agreeable to her own."

NOTE C.

"To the Marchioness de La Fayette.

"Mount Vernon, 25 November, 1784.

"Madam:

"If my expressions were equal to my sensibility, I should, in more elegant language than I am master of, declare to you my sense of the obligation I am under for the letter you did me the honor to write to me by the Marquis de La Fayette, and thanks for this flattering instance of your regard. The pleasure I received in once more embracing my friend could only have been increased by your presence, and the opportunity I should thereby have had of paying, in my own house, the homage of my respectful attachment to his better half. I have the promise, which the Marquis has ratified to Mrs. Washington, that he will use his influence to bring you with him to this country, whenever he shall visit it again. When the weight of so powerful an advocate is on your side, will you, my dear Marchioness, deny us the pleasure of your accompanying him to the shores of Columbia? In offering our mite, we can only assure you, that endeavors shall not be wanting on our part to make this new world as agreeable to you, as rural scenes and peaceful retirement are competent to.

"The Marquis returns to you with all the warmth and ardor of a newly-inspired lover. We restore him to you in good health, crowned with wreaths of love and respect from every part of the Union. That his meeting with you, his family, and friends may be propitious, and as happy as your wishes can make it, that you may live long together revered and beloved, and that you may transmit to a numerous progeny the virtues which you both possess, is the fervent wish of your devoted and

"Most respectful

"Humble servant,

"GEORGE WASHINGTON.

"N. B. In every good wish for you, Mrs. Washington sincerely joins me."

Accompanying this letter was the following epistle, addressed to the little Virginia de La Fayette, which, though it has no direct connection with our subject, is too interesting and characteristic to be separated from its companion:—

"To Mademoiselle de La Fayette.

"Mount Vernon, 25 November, 1784.

"Permit me to thank my dear little correspondent for the favor of her letter of the 18 of June last, and to impress her with the idea of the pleasure I shall derive from a continuance of them. Her papa is restored to her with all the good health, paternal affection, and honors, which her tender heart could wish. He will carry a kiss to her from me (which might be more agreeable from a pretty boy), and give her assurances of the affectionate regard with which I have the pleasure of being her well-wisher.

"George Washington."

"To the Marchioness de La Fayette.

"Mount Vernon, 10 May, 1786.

"Madam:

"The tokens of regard, with which Miss de La Fayette and my namesake* honored the young folks of this family, will cement the friendship, which seems to be rising in their tender hearts, and will increase those flames of it, which they have imbibed from their parents, to which nothing

* George Washington La Fayette.

can add strength but the endearments that flow from personal interviews, and the unreserved exchange of liberal sentiments. Will you not then, Madam, afford them this opportunity? May we hope for it soon? If the assurances of the sincerest esteem and affection, if the varieties of uncultivated nature, the novelty of exchanging the gay and delightful scenes of Paris, with which you are surrounded, for the rural amusements of a country in its infancy; if the warbling notes of the feathered songsters on our lawns and meads, can for a moment make you forget the melody of the opera and the pleasures of the court, these all invite you to give us this honor, and the opportunity of expressing to you personally those sentiments of attachment and love, with which you have inspired us.

"The noontide of life is now passed with Mrs. Washington and myself; and all we have to do is to spend the evening of our days in tranquillity, and glide gently down a stream which no human effort can ascend. We must, therefore, however reluctantly it is done, forgo the pleasure of such a visit as you kindly invite us to make. But the case with you is far otherwise. Your days are in their meridian brightness. In the natural order of things, you have many years to come, in which you may indulge yourself in all the amusements, which variety can afford, and different countries produce, and in receiving those testimonies of respect which every one in the United States would wish to render to you.

"My mother will receive the compliments you honor her with, as flattering marks of attention; and I shall have great pleasure in delivering them myself. My best wishes and vows are offered for you, and for the fruits of your love; and with every sentiment of respect and attachment,

"I have the honor to be, Madam, &c.

"GEORGE WASHINGTON."*

* Sparks' PRIVATE LETTERS OF WASHINGTON.

NOTE D.

"THE EARL OF BUCHAN TO MRS. WASHINGTON

"Dryburgh Abbey, Jan. 28, 1800.

"MADAM:

"I have this day received from my brother, at London, the afflicting tidings of the death of your admirable husband, my revered kinsman and friend. I am not afraid, even under this sudden and unexpected stroke of Divine Providence, to give vent to the immediate reflections excited by it, because my attachment to your illustrious consort was the pure result of reason, reflection, and congeniality of sentiment. He was one of those whom the Almighty, in successive ages, has chosen and raised up to promote the ultimate designs of his goodness and mercy, in the gradual melioration of his creatures and the coming of his kingdom, which is in heaven.

"It may be said of this great and good man who has been taken from among us, what was written by the wise and discerning Tacitus concerning his father-in-law Agricola, that, "though he was snatched away while his age was not broken by infirmity or dimmed by bodily decay of reason, yet that, if his life be measured by his glory, he attained to a mighty length of days; for every true felicity, namely, all such as arise from virtue, he had already enjoyed to the full. As he had likewise held the supreme authority of the state with the confidence and applause of all wise and good men in every part of the world, as well as among those he governed, and had enjoyed triumphal honors in a war undertaken for the defence of the inalienable rights of mankind, what more, humanly speaking, could fortune add to his lustre and renown?"

"After enormous wealth he sought not; an honorable share he possessed. His course he finished in the peaceful retreat of his own election, in the arms of a dutiful and affectionate wife, and bedewed with the tears of surrounding relatives and friends, with the unspeakably superior advantage to that of a Roman general, in the hopes afforded by the Gospel of pardon and peace! He therefore, Madam, to continue my parallel, may be accounted singularly happy, since by dying according to his own Christian and humble wish, expressed on many occasions, while his credit was nowise impaired, his fame in all its splendor, nis relations and friends not only in a state of comfort and security, but of honor, he was probably to escape many evils incident to declining years. Moreover, he saw the government of his country in hands conformable to our joint wishes and to the safety of the nation, and a contingent succession opening, not less favorable to the liberties and happiness of the people.

"Considering my uniform regard for the American States, manifested long before their forming a separate nation, I may be classed as it were among their citizens, especially as I am come of a worthy ancestor, Lord Cardross, who found refuge there in the last century, and had large property in Carolina, where Port Royal is now situated. I hope it will not be thought impertinent or officious, if I recommend to that country and nation of America at large the constant remembrance of the moral and political maxims conveyed to its citizens by the Father and Founder of the United States, in his farewell address, in that speech which he made to the Senate and House of Representatives, where the last hand was put to the formation of the Federal Constitution; *and may it be perpetual.*

"It seems to me that such maxims and such

advice ought to be engraved on every forum or place of common assembly among the people, and read by parents, teachers, and guardians to their children and pupils, so that true religion, and virtue, its inseparable attendant, may be imbibed by the rising generation to remote ages; and the foundations of national policy be laid and continued in the superstructure, in the pure and immutable principles of private morality, since there is no truth more thoroughly established than that there exists in the economy and course of nature an indissoluble union between virtue and happiness, between duty and happiness, between duty and advantage, between the genuine maxims of an honest and magnanimous people, and the solid rewards of public prosperity and felicity; since we ought to be no less persuaded that the propitious smiles of heaven can never be expected on a nation that disregards the eternal rules of order and right which Heaven itself has ordained; and since the preservation of the sacred fire of liberty and the destiny of the Republican model of government are justly considered as deeply, perhaps finally, staked on the experiment entrusted to the hands of the American people.

"Lady Buchan joins with me in the most sincere, respectful good wishes.

"I am, Madam, with sincere esteem,

"Your obedient and faithful servant,

"BUCHAN."

NOTE E.

After some particulars in relation to the several churches in the vicinity of Mount Vernon, the fair writer gives us the following interesting details respecting Washington and family:—

"We attended the Church at Alexandria, when the weather and roads permitted a ride of ten miles. In New York and Philadelphia, he never omitted attendance at church in the morning, unless detained by indisposition. The afternoon was spent in his own room at home; the evening with his family and without company. Sometimes an old and intimate friend called to see us for an hour or two; but visiting and visitors were prohibited for that day. No one in church attended to the services with more reverential respect. My grandmother, who was eminently pious, never deviated from her usual habits. She always knelt. The general, as was then the custom, stood during the devotional parts of the service. On communion Sundays, he left the church with me, after the blessing, and returned home, and we sent the carriage back for my grandmother.

"It was his custom to retire to his library at nine or ten o'clock, where he remained an hour before he went to his chamber. He always rose before the sun, and remained in his library until called to breakfast. I never *witnessed* his private devotions, I never *inquired* about them. I should have thought it the greatest heresy to doubt his firm belief in Christianity. His life, his writings, prove that he was a Christian. He was not one of those who act, or pray, 'that they may be seen of men.' He communed with his God in secret.

"My mother resided two years at Mount Vernon, after her marriage with John Park Custis, the only son of Mrs. Washington. I have heard her say that General Washington always received the sacrament with my grandmother before the Revolution. When my aunt, Miss Custis, died suddenly at Mount Vernon, before they could realize the event, he knelt by her and prayed most fervently, most affectingly for her recovery. Of this I was assured by Judge Washington's mother, and other witnesses.

"He was a silent, thoughtful man. He spoke little generally; never of himself. I never heard him relate a single act of his life during the war. I have often seen him perfectly abstracted, his lips moving, but no sound was perceptible. I have often made him laugh most heartily from sympathy with my joyous and extravagant spirits. I was, probably, one of the last persons on earth to whom he would have addressed serious conversation, particularly when he knew that I had the most perfect model of female excellence ever with me as my monitress, who acted the part of a tender and devoted parent, loving me only as a mother can love, and never extenuating or approving in me what she disapproved in others. She never omitted her private devotions, or her public duties; and she and her husband were so perfectly united and happy that he must have been a Christian. She had no doubts, no fears, for him. After forty years of devoted affection and uninterrupted happiness, she resigned him without a murmur into the arms of his Saviour and his God, with the assured hope of his eternal felicity."

THE END.

Headley's Women of the Bible: Historical and descriptive sketches of the Women of the Bible, as maidens, wives, and mothers; from Eve of the Old, to the Marys of the New Testament: by Rev. P. C. Headley, in one 12mo. volume, illustrated — uniform with "Headley's Sacred Mountains." $1,25.

The author of this work possesses enough traits of resemblance to the author of the Sacred Mountains, to leave no doubt of his right to the name of Headley. There is much of that spirited descriptive power, which has made the elder brother a popular favorite, and gives promise of a successful career on his own account. The sketches are brief, and embody all the historic incidents recorded of them.—*New York Evangelist.*

A younger brother of J. T. Headley is the author of this beautiful volume. It will probably have a larger circulation than the splendid work issued last fall by the Messrs. Appleton, being better adapted for the general reader, in form and price, while it is ornamental enough for the centre table. It contains nineteen descriptive biographical sketches, arranged in chronological order, including nearly all the distinguished women of the sacred annals, and forming an outline of Scripture history. The illustrations are from original designs, and are numerous and appropriate. No ordinary powers of imagination and expression are shown in the vivid and picturesque descriptions; and the fine portraitures of character rivet the interest, and set forth the Scripture delineations in a stronger light. In this respect the book has no rival, for no other is so complete, following so closely at the same time, the sacred narrative. We hope it is but an earnest of other works from the pen of its gifted author.—*Home Journal.*

We were so struck with the title of this work, and the prepossessing appearance of its typography, that we have so far departed from the usual course adopted in like cases, as to *read* carefully the work in hand, before recommending it to our readers. And we are prepared to say, that a more attractive volume has not fallen in our way for a long time. It is made up of brief historical and descriptive eulogies of the most remarkable females of a most extraordinary era in the world's history. The author has appropriated very much of the poetry and romance of the Bible, in the sketches he has given of *nineteen* women, who have come down to us through their peculiar merits, embalmed in sacred inspiration. Whoever reads the story of Sarah, the beautiful Hebrew maiden, the admiration of the Chaldean shepherds and the pride of her kindred; or of Rebecca, whom the "faithful steward of Abraham" journeyed to the land of Nahor and selected as the bride of Isaac, and who, it is said, "was *very fair to look upon;*" or of Rachel, the beautiful shepherdess who tended her father's flocks in the valley of Haran; or of Merriam, Deborah, Jeptha's Daughter, Delilah, Ruth, Queen of Sheba, the Shunamite, Esther, Elizabeth, Virgin Mary, Dorcas, and others — will read a story far more interesting and attractive than any romance or novel. Every young lady in town should read this work; and we will venture to say that they *will* do so if they but once get hold of it, for it is a book that cannot be laid aside.— *Oswego Times.*

History of the War with Mexico, from the commencement of hostilities with the United States, to the ratification of Peace; embracing detailed accounts of the brilliant achievements of Generals Taylor, Scott, Worth, Wool, Twiggs, Kearney, and others; by John S. Jenkins, 8vo., 20 illustrations, morocco gilt. $2,50.

A History of the late war prepared for popular circulation The writer takes a patriotic view of his subject. His narrative of the commencement of the war would, we presume, not displease Mr. Polk. He follows the campaign throughout with industry and spirit, drawing from public documents, diplomatic correspondence, and the newspaper letter writers by the way. More facts, we believe, are brought together than in any single publication of the kind. The narratives of adventure in California, Col. Doniphan's march, and other passages, are told with interest; the writer evidently seeking to make a useful book. The portraits and illustrations of scenes are numerous; the mechanical execution of the whole work being highly creditable to the Auburn publishers.—*Literary World.*

This is a volume of over 500 pages. The publishers have brought it out in excellent style. The paper, type, printing and binding, are admirable. The book has been written with due regard to accuracy, and in a popular style. It is the most elaborate, and probably the best History of the War yet published.—*Albany Evening Journal.*

We have been unable to notice, until now, this new work from the pen of the author of " The Generals of the last War with Great Britain, etc." In this volume we have at last a complete and interesting history of the late collision between the two Republics of the Continent. To a minute and detailed account of the position and policy of Mexico, the origin and causes of War, are added soul-stirring descriptions of the brilliant and successful engagements of our army with the enemy. This narrative is written after a careful examination of the diplomatic correspondence and the various publications, of a public or private character, that have appeared from time to time, calculated to throw light on the subject. To render the work still more interesting and desirable, it has been illustrated with portraits of the most distinguished officers of our own and the Mexican army, with views of the ever memorable battle-fields of Buena Vista and Cerro Gordo. The reputation of the author will insure for this history a very general circulation.—*Albany Atlas.*

www.ingramcontent.com/pod-product-compliance
Lightning Source LLC
LaVergne TN
LVHW010250110826
845151LV00004B/1435

* 9 7 8 1 4 2 5 5 2 3 6 1 9 *